I0797952

Any Given Moment

52 Devotions and Prayers
to Feel the Goodness of God

Sarah Molitor

A Tyndale nonfiction imprint

Visit Tyndale online at tyndale.com.

Visit Tyndale Momentum online at tyndalemomentum.com.

Visit the author online at modernfarmhousefamily.com.

Tyndale, Tyndale's quill logo, *Tyndale Momentum*, and the Tyndale Momentum logo are registered trademarks of Tyndale House Ministries. Tyndale Momentum is a nonfiction imprint of Tyndale House Publishers, Carol Stream, Illinois.

Any Given Moment: 52 Devotions and Prayers to Feel the Goodness of God

Cover design by Eva M. Winters

Interior design by Laura Cruise

For information about special discounts for bulk purchases, please contact Tyndale House Publishers at csresponse@tyndale.com, or call 1-800-323-9400.

Library of Congress Cataloging-in-Publication Data

A catalog record for this book is available from the Library of Congress.

ISBN 978-1-4964-7177-2

Printed in China

31 30 29 28 27 26 25
7 6 5 4 3 2 1

Dear Mom (and the world's greatest Nana),

This devotional is dedicated to you. Do you realize that you have impacted countless women with your encouragement? The number of women whose lives have been changed because of you giving of your time and love is uncountable. You've made it your mission to love big behind the scenes.

Thanks for teaching me how to encourage others through my writing. I'm a better everything (even a better writer) because of you, and I want to always do the same for others as you have modeled for me. God couldn't have given me a better mom. I love you so much!

—Your favorite (and only) redheaded daughter

Contents

Introduction ... 1

When I Need to Be Rescued ... 5
He Never Fails Us ... 9
The Invisible Backpack ... 13
Stay Vigilant ... 17
Knowing His Voice ... 21
Share Your Burdens ... 25
Hidden in Our Hearts ... 31
New Vision ... 35
From the Inside Out ... 41
Strong and Courageous ... 45
Cheerleader ... 51
Practice Peace ... 55
Rest in the Lord ... 59
Forward in Faith ... 63
God Still Works Miracles ... 69
Things Will Still Bloom ... 75
A Dream Come True ... 79
What Is God Like? ... 85
Don't Be an End Cap ... 91
The Joy of Flexibility ... 95
K.W.U.F. ... 99
Reason to Rejoice ... 103
God Looks at the Heart ... 107
Fighting Fear ... 111
Touchpoints ... 115
The Bigger Picture ... 119

Solid Rock ... 123
Made to Work ... 127
Pray for a Daniel ... 133
An Open Invitation ... 139
The Right Environment ... 143
With All Your Heart ... 149
God-Given Identity ... 153
Build Each Other Up ... 157
The Power of Self-Control ... 163
Clean Out Your Heart ... 167
Be a Gatekeeper ... 171
A Lasting Legacy ... 175
Delight in the Lord ... 179
Words of Life ... 183
Would've, Should've, Could've ... 189
Hard to Love ... 193
Close to the Brokenhearted ... 199
Healthy Habits ... 205
Choose True Joy ... 211
Step Out in Faith ... 217
Play Offense ... 223
Team Jesus ... 229
In Christ Alone ... 235
Clothed with Strength and Dignity ... 241
Check Engine Light ... 247
No Regrets ... 253

Acknowledgments ... 257
Index ... 260
About the Author ... 263

Introduction

AT THE TIME, I DIDN'T REALIZE how special it would become. I just prayed because it felt like the right response in that moment. Truthfully, it's always the right response, even though I sometimes forget to take my own advice. But after that first Sunday that I prayed out loud with my online community, I started receiving messages full of prayer requests. And I quickly felt as though the Lord asked me to keep going. So I did. Each week, I opened my social media and asked the Lord to make His words my words and to speak through me. This weekly commitment to pray with others quickly became a favorite priority in my life. Now, any given Sunday evening you can still find me ducking away from whatever is happening to go pray with friends I may never meet. Friends like each of you! But if we never meet and I never fully know these friends, why do it? Because we are connected by the Lord and His faithfulness. Because God isn't confined to time or place and is touching lives even through an app. Because prayers are being answered—often quickly and sometimes over longer spans of time with consistent prayer. Because if I could share with you the testimonies that others have shared with me, you would be instantly encouraged in your faith! And because even those who don't recognize God as their Lord and Savior just yet are drawn to His love through prayer.

The Lord began to put on my heart a desire for this encouragement, this prayer time, to have a permanent place. Not just in some virtual cloud or highlight reel but on paper, where it could be read and recited over and over to keep His promises at the forefront of our hearts. Like the Lord says in Habakkuk 2:2, "Write my answer plainly on tablets, so that a runner can carry the correct message to others."

I want to be the runner. Not the kind that runs marathons (trust me on this one). But the kind that runs to carry the correct message of Christ to the hearts of others so they can hear and know His goodness too. I know from personal experience that encouraging words and prayers spoken to me in specific seasons have brought not only comfort but a challenge to press into the Lord more and seek His ways and will for my life.

I hope the words you read in this book bring the same feelings for you. As I began to write, I created a simple template for myself to follow—one that I surveyed my sisters and mom for to learn what they loved in devotional books they had read. I combined all of our favorite elements to create the structure for each week's devotional. In every one, you will find a verse to think on for that day or week, an encouragement that may include personal stories as well as a biblical foundation, a simple yet actionable step to carry into the week ahead, and a prayer to read and meditate on. There's also a topical index at the back of the book for those days you need a specific encouraging word for your circumstances.

Words can be hard. But prayer shouldn't be. And my hope is that as you read and pray your way through these pages, God will speak to you through His Word. I pray my written words will simply be a vessel for the Lord to speak directly to your spirit, exactly how you need. And that, with each reading, you will feel comforted, valued, seen, encouraged, and challenged.

I'm so thankful for you as my friend. Without you and the Lord, this devotional wouldn't be here, and I believe with all my heart that these words and prayers will have an eternal impact for God's Kingdom. May it be so!

In complete thankfulness,

Sarah

In His good timing that often doesn't make sense to us, He answers.

1

When I Need to Be Rescued

The LORD says, "I will rescue those who love me.
I will protect those who trust in my name."

PSALM 91:14

I DON'T NEED TO BE RESCUED. That's how I felt, at least. Because in that moment, five years into marriage, as much as I knew I wanted to change the unkind way I spoke to my husband, I figured I could do the changing myself. Until I realized I couldn't, no matter how hard I tried. So when that option dead-ended, I figured I would give God a shot at doing the rescuing. He might know a thing or two about that, given His history. Not so shockingly, He came through. *And He's continued to come through ever since.*

About three years ago, my sister-in-law's heart stopped a few hours after giving birth. No explanation. No warning. No answers. She needed to be rescued. Yet thousands of miles away and across an ocean, what could I possibly do? So I asked God to do the rescuing. We asked and prayed and pleaded and trusted. Three months later, she walked out of those hospital doors with answers and healing. *And He's continued to come through ever since.*

Then there was the time our sixth son was sick. Night after night, day after day, he got no relief and struggled to breathe. We did everything we could to help. He needed to be rescued. Yet no medicine, no oil, nothing we tried seemed to make a difference. So in the depths of the night, rocking back and forth, tears streaming down my face, I once again asked God for rescue. I knew He could because He had proven Himself faithful. In the dark of that room, peace covered us like a blanket as we rocked. *And He's continued to come through ever since.*

Faithful. Good. Steady. Rescuer. Protector.

One of the verses I repeated out loud through tears when my son was sick was Psalm 91:14. The funny part about it is that I'd memorized it by happenstance. I had been helping my boys memorize Bible verses for a challenge my parents gave them. Each day for two months, we would practice a verse or two and slowly put them together. I didn't think much of it at the time.

But then those nights came. The nights when he was so sick and I was so exhausted that I didn't know what else to do. When I had nothing else to pray and nowhere else to turn, I knew I needed to turn upward. The words that came off my lips were from Psalm 91:14: "The Lord says, 'I will rescue those who love me. I will protect those who trust in my name.'"

I'm not saying we will always get the answers we want or think we need, but the good news is *He* is the answer. Whatever question you have, whatever prayer you pray, whatever tears you cry, *He answers*. In His good timing that often doesn't make sense to us, He answers. In His good ways that sometimes don't look so good from our perspective, He answers. God is in the unique business of rescuing and protecting, but there is another part of Psalm 91:14 that is important also.

"I will rescue *those who love me*."

"I will protect *those who trust in my name*."

When you are in a relationship with another person, it's only fair that each side puts forth some effort. This is also true of our relationship with God. *Love Him. Trust Him.* Know that even when things look bleak and don't go the way we hoped, His way is better than the paths we plotted and the prayers we prayed for ourselves.

The requests and prayers we send up to heaven can often be as loaded as a baked potato. (Not sure why that came to mind—maybe I'm hungry!) When God doesn't answer our prayers in the exact way we hoped, we may feel discouraged or let down. But once we have the benefit of hindsight, sometimes we will see how His hand was directing our situation the whole time. God truly never leaves us. He just asks us to love Him and trust in His name.

So here I am. I've lived a little bit of life, and I can tell you from that little bit that doing what God asks is worth whatever risk you might perceive.

To love God is *to allow* Him to be our rescuer.

To trust in His name is *to know* He will be our protector.

Once we release those two jobs from our grip, we find the freedom to live in Him, knowing He will do it. Once you know that, it's a lot easier to remember the next time that He always comes through.

Let's walk forward into this week trusting in the Lord to protect and rescue us so we can give Him all the glory in every situation we face.

Pray

Dear Lord, thank You so much that You have chosen to rescue me again and again. Whether or not I've noticed it, You have always come through for me. Lord, help me to not look to You just when I'm desperate but to look to You at all times. I trust in Your name, and I trust in the path and plans You have laid out for my life. Help me to walk securely in them because of my trust in You. Protect me along the way and be my defender and rescuer every minute of every day. Lord, I love You, and I ask You to forgive me for the times I've tried to do life all on my own. Thank You for going before me, being with me right now, and always covering me. In Jesus' name, amen.

Whatever comes, may our first response be "Hallelujah!"

2

He Never Fails Us

Be strong and courageous! Do not be afraid and do not panic before them. For the LORD your God will personally go ahead of you. He will neither fail you nor abandon you.

DEUTERONOMY 31:6

I WILL NEVER FORGET the moment Tim called me in a panic and said, "Please pray! My dad just collapsed and I'm going to the hospital with him right now." Not much could have prepared us for what followed. In that instant, our lives changed forever. Four days later, in the hospital, we were having conversations that no one wants to have, laying out all the what-ifs as if we were playing some game. Yet it wasn't a game, and we were very aware of that. We knew decisions needed to be made, though we also knew that God had Tim's dad's days and years planned out already. It was confusing and overwhelming.

As everyone was preparing for the worst, suddenly, in the middle of the uncertainty, hope inserted itself. Within less than a day, Tim's dad went from completely unconscious to awake and responsive to commands. But that was only the first hurdle. He was diagnosed with a massive stroke, and as we have continued to walk this uncertain road over the past eight years, we've learned many lessons laced with God's steadiness and faithfulness.

One of these lessons is how God never fails us or leaves us. What a gift He personally goes ahead of us, just as the Bible says He will. He never abandons us, just as He promises. We do nothing to deserve any of it, yet God lavishes His goodness on our lives, often in unexpected and "I didn't see that coming" ways. And that's exactly what He did during this family medical crisis. It's nothing we would have planned or asked for. And it's been anything but easy.

But want to know something really cool about this story? Before his stroke, Tim's dad would say "Hallelujah" (Praise the Lord) as if it were applicable to everything in life. It was his hello and goodbye. His word that covered everything. We'd be having a tough time, and he would say, "Well, hallelujah; you guys will know what to do." Or we'd be thrilled about some news, and he would say, "Hallelujah! This is so exciting." He was so certain of who God is that you could feel it every time he uttered the word. So it only seems fitting that when he woke up from that stroke, sat up for the first time, and looked around, his first word was none other than "Hallelujah."

He lost so much from his stroke. We all felt like we did too. But his "hallelujah" has never left him, and that's something I want to take on for myself. To have a heavenly perspective even when my world is shaking. And to respond to that shaking with a firm "hallelujah." May I be grounded enough to rest in praising God through all the seasons that threaten to shake me up. May I be "strong and courageous" as Deuteronomy 31:6 says, not afraid or full of panic, because I know that I know that I know that God personally goes ahead of me in everything.

Let's walk forward into this week so rooted in Christ that any shaking in our life makes our roots go deeper into what God has for us. Whatever comes, may our first response be "Hallelujah!"

Pray

Dear Lord, my world feels like it's being shaken right now. Certain areas are getting the best of me and weighing me down. It honestly feels unfair. Lord, right now I need You to be the faithful God You have always been to me. I'm asking You to please continue that! I need You to carry me right now and show Yourself faithful in my life. I offer You what I'm struggling with, and through it all I say, "Hallelujah!" and "Help me!" God, I know I tend to hold tightly to things in my life. But I want to give them to You, knowing that You will hold them even tighter and care for me through it all. Lord, I give You my marriage, my children, my friendships, my job, my health. All of it—it's Yours. Would You replace my anxiety with peace? Would You move in my life and transform all the parts that need work? Don't let me get in my own way or in the way of a breakthrough You have for me. I need You to go before me and steady me in all I'm facing. I need Your perspective. Thank You for Your faithfulness to me, Lord. I know You are there—I'm counting on it. Hallelujah! In Jesus' name, amen.

God cares for us, so He carries our burdens.

3

The Invisible Backpack

Give all your worries and cares to God, for he cares about you.

1 PETER 5:7

I REMEMBER THIS ONE NIGHT (okay, maybe there has been more than one) where nothing I did felt good enough. It had been a day, and I wanted to be recognized for all my contributions to getting through it. Everything I did that day seemed to add weight to an invisible backpack that grew heavier by the hour. When dinner came and went and no compliments or thank-yous followed from my children or my husband, I lost it. The first thing I lost was a good attitude and a right heart. Once that was gone, I let my exhaustion take over. And for my grand finale, I began dumping out all my invisible burdens for everyone to hear. Not exactly my most shining moment.

Once all was said and done and the kids were asleep, I plopped onto my bed, worn down. I was exhausted from carrying around a whole day's worth of invisible burdens and letting my feelings take over. Instead of looking to the Lord in my tired moments and crying, "Help!," I let the weight of the day get the better of me. As I lay there, I knew I had gotten it all wrong. Maybe you know the feeling.

Not so shockingly, after a good night's sleep and some food, it was amazing how different I felt. Tim always tells me I won't solve any problems when I'm hungry, tired, or it's after 10 p.m., yet somehow I always think I will. But the truth is that I won't solve any problems when I'm busy trying to be the problem solver instead of letting the Lord do what He does best. Instead of casting my cares on Him, I decide that carrying all the burdens of whatever happens to and around me is a great idea. Can you imagine if we all wore see-through backpacks every day? We would start our day with empty backpacks and slowly add bricks for every burden or mishap we faced. Then we would carry our bricks from our house to the grocery store and back to our house. Maybe to our office or down the stairs, outside, and to the car. Backpacking them into church on Sundays.

It's a laughable picture, right? Yet it's all too easy to live this way. We think we are "managing" or "balancing" things well. After all, I can carry bricks better than you, right? I know how to stack them just right so they don't make me fall over. Until they do. And my world crumbles. But that is *not* what God designed for us.

We are never meant to carry that kind of weight. Why do we try? Control. The more I can control the ins and outs of my day, the more in control I feel—only to discover that I'm just one brick away from being tipped over. So here we have this picture of us carrying around the weight of all these things we deem important, but on the other side of heaven we have a gracious God offering to off-load our bricks. Now notice this: our key verse today doesn't say, "Give all your worries and cares to God and He will make them disappear." No, that's not the promise. The promise is that God cares for us, so He carries our burdens. He off-loads them from us and carries them for us while we walk with Him.

Letting God have control over even the smallest areas of our lives actually frees us from being weighed down. The coolest part of it all to me? When our backpacks are emptied, we have a big, empty space for the Lord to pour into and show us how He would have us live. At the end of chapter 11 of the book of Matthew, Jesus says, "Come to me, all you who are weary and burdened, and I will give you rest. Take my yoke upon you and learn from me, for I am gentle and humble in heart, and you will find rest for your souls. For my yoke is easy and my burden is light" (verses 28-30, NIV). I don't know about you, but I can guess that most of us would gladly exchange whatever we carry around daily for a burden that is much, much lighter. And that isn't just something that sounds nice—it's a promise from Jesus.

So let's take the Lord up on His promises today. No more endless exhaustion. Let's cast our cares on Him, drop our bricks at the door, and say, "Have Your way, Lord!" (One more thing: when we do this, let's not forget to go back and ask forgiveness from anyone we might have dropped a brick on along the way!)

Let's walk forward into this week knowing that next time we're carrying a burden, we can choose to cast it quickly on Jesus and exchange it for His gentleness and rest.

Pray

Dear Lord, there are some days when I feel downright tired—exhausted from all the things I've let build up inside and outside of me. I ask that in the midst of the exhaustion, You would remind me that my words and actions still matter. I want to remember that even in the middle of my weariness, I can come to You. Even when life feels hard or heavy, I can come to You and offer You what I have—and You will fill in the gaps. I pray that in the moments I feel "less than," I would turn to You first. God, nothing is too big for You. I proclaim that my life is Yours, and that means even the tired moments. It's Your strength, Lord, that sustains me. I want to be faithful because I know You are faithful to take whatever burdens I carry. In Jesus' name, amen.

God's plans are so good, they're worth battling for!

4

Stay Vigilant

Stay alert! Watch out for your great enemy, the devil. He prowls around like a roaring lion, looking for someone to devour.

1 PETER 5:8

I DON'T LIKE BEING CAUGHT OFF GUARD. I like to be prepared, so much so that I'll start packing for a trip three or four days before we leave, and that's after I've spent weeks making lists, doing laundry, slowly laying out items we may need. I remember one trip in particular. We were going away for six days for me to speak at my first conference. My topic? Using our words well. I fully prepared everything, packing for our seven children and myself. (My husband took five minutes to throw a couple of T-shirts, boxers, and a pair of pants in a suitcase and proclaimed he was ready. It always seems so much easier for him!) Then I filled their backpacks, each of which contained a game or two, a book, headphones, and a large bag of snacks. Never forget the snacks! By the time I was done, I was pretty proud of myself. A few days later, we flew more than halfway across the country and drove a bit more to make it to our destination.

That final drive to our rental was a drive to remember. Maybe you know the kind? The baby was screaming, our two-year-old was tired, and we took about four wrong turns, extending our drive time by half an hour down a rocky forest road that was mostly uninhabited. You still with me? At this point, I let loose. And by loose, I mean all the wrong words came out.

Later that evening, at our final destination, I was so frustrated with how I'd acted. *Why, Lord, would You bring me here to encourage others on how to use their words when I can't even keep my own attitude together?* As we unpacked and I shared these thoughts with my parents, my dad said, "Well, what did you expect? For it to be all smooth sailing?" I guess, yes! I did expect that. But as they spoke, I was reminded that we live in a fallen world. A world with an enemy who would love nothing more than to see us lose everything . . . even ourselves.

But in the same thought, I was also reminded that we need to stay vigilant. As believers, our lives are marked with God's calling. And the enemy—the devil—wants nothing more than to "steal and kill and destroy" (John 10:10). He's already lost, so he would love for us to lose with him. To lose our tempers, our words, our relationships, our marriages, our children, our everything. Because if he can win in any of those areas, he knows it weakens a piece of us. And he will do it however he can. Strife, stress, sickness, discontentment, discouragement, disappointment. It doesn't matter how we fail as long as we do!

However, we have an antidote to these attacks: the Word of God. God's Word is our ultimate authority. Isaiah 54:17 assures us that when we use the tools God gives us—the Word of God and the armor of God— "no weapon turned against [us] will succeed." My battle is not against my husband or my children or my situation. The Word of God tells us in Ephesians 6:12 that "we are not fighting against flesh-and-blood enemies, but against evil rulers and authorities of the unseen world, against mighty powers in this dark world, and against evil spirits in the heavenly places."

I want to be aware of what battles I'm fighting day in and day out yet also alert to what battles may lie ahead. If I know I'm about to do something the Lord has orchestrated, I better also be fully aware that the enemy isn't going to sit idly by and watch God's Kingdom grow and be impacted for good without trying to stop it! The devil will do his darndest to keep me out of step. And he'll do that to you too.

I want to be a vigilant believer. Don't you? The kind of believer who knows the omnipotence of the God we serve but is also aware of the enemy's tricks and lies. Go back and read the verse at the beginning of this devo one more time. God wants us to be on guard so His Kingdom will be glorified.

Let's walk forward into this week aware and alert—but also excited to know that God's plans are so good, they're worth battling for!

Pray

Dear Lord, help me to be aware of Your presence and Your purposes while also being aware of the devil's devices to divide and cause messes. I want to be on guard and alert in my life so I can point out the enemy's schemes and defeat them with the name of Jesus! Help me to know Your Word so I can use it in a real and strong way to fight off the lies and deception that the devil tries to weave into my life. God, I declare that the enemy has no hold on my life, but You have ultimate authority in all You do. I'm so thankful for that. I pray that You would protect me and help me to come to You as a refuge. Lord, let me also be a light for others to see Your saving grace in their own lives. I don't want to just live for myself—I want to preach Your name boldly, knowing that there is nothing the enemy hates more. Help me to do all these things in Your strength. In Jesus' name, amen.

In order
to hear God,
we must
know Him.

5

Knowing His Voice

Jesus replied "But even more blessed are all who hear the word of God and put it into practice."

LUKE 11:28

ONE OF MY KIDS' FAVORITE BOOKS is about three knights trying to complete a challenge to win the hand of a princess. In the book, a prince explains that the challenge is to cross a dangerous forest and make it to the castle on the other side. Each knight can pick one companion. And every day, morning and night, the king in the castle will play a song on his flute to guide them through the forest. The prince plays the song for the knights so they know its sound. As all the knights consider whom to take, one knight asks if anyone else plays the king's song. The prince says no. Each knight chooses his companion and goes on his way.

After several days, only one knight and his companion emerge, beaten and tattered, from the forest. Can you guess how this knight did it? He chose the right companion: the prince. As the knight and the prince traveled, the creatures of the forest tried to imitate the king's song and get the knight off course. But the prince played the true song over and over, so the winning knight knew the sound to follow each day.

Isn't this story such a picture of following God and hearing His voice? Our world is jam-packed full of voices trying to imitate God and His Word. Instead of God's truth, our culture emphasizes "my truth." God's voice seems muffled by the noise of our everyday lives. It's easy to choose wrong companions who will lead us astray and get us off course. But don't buy into that lie, friends. Jesus is the only companion who can keep us on track.

God has a distinct voice and wants to *actively* speak into our lives. The Holy Spirit is just waiting for us to tap into the everyday nudges and discernment that are all part of following Jesus. But in order to hear God, we must know Him. We must root ourselves into relationship the same way we would when we meet a new friend and invite them to our home. As we spend time with them, we learn things we didn't know before. I have some dear friends I've known for years, but I'm still learning new things about them. After seven years of friendship, I invited one of my friends to an amusement park only to find out she never goes because she gets so sick on rides. I had no clue. And that's just a simple example of learning something new. I know the learning won't stop.

God is the same way! The more we read the Bible, the more we see His character and understand His goodness, the more we get to know Him! This means we will recognize His distinct voice in our lives and how He speaks to us. Knowing His voice will help us discern when other voices try to creep in and cloud our thoughts. We know something is from the Lord when it is backed up by the Word of God. That should always be our measuring stick.

The devil isn't stupid, but we have to remember that if we are in Christ, he has no power over us. My dad always says, "The devil only has a few tricks, but he will use them over and over to try to trip us up." He'll use fear and doubt to make us question our decisions; he will use strife and disagreement to fuel arguments; he'll even use our past to make us question our future. Basically, he lights a fire, and we fuel it when we let these things take hold in our lives. So I want to learn to recognize them for what they are. We need to call them out as false and squelch the fire before the flames get out of hand. How do we do that? I'll say it again: in order to hear God, we must know Him. Really, really know Him. And then we need to practice listening. When we read the Bible, I want to challenge us to ask questions like "What are You saying here, God?" or "God, what does this tell me about Your character?" As we do that, I believe we will begin to experience a more active two-way relationship with God—which is really exciting!

Let's walk forward into this week asking God to help us discern His voice clearly and to help us know Him so well that we aren't led astray by imitators or distractors but instead stay on the path He has laid out for us.

Pray

Dear Lord, Thank You for Your voice in my life! You are the One who speaks truth and life and encouragement. When I am at a low point, it's easy to hear all the noise and sometimes hard to hear from You. Please help me to know You more each day so I can discern Your voice in my life with confidence. Settle in my Spirit who You are so that amid everything else going on, I hear You first! I want to know You, Lord. I want to know Your voice the same way I know a friend's voice. I ask for clarity as I turn to You, attuning myself to Your voice. I want to hear from You, and I invite You into every situation, whether mundane or momentous. In Jesus' name, amen.

Let's
not be
stubborn
about
needing
the Lord.

6

Share Your Burdens

God is our refuge and strength, always
ready to help in times of trouble.

PSALM 46:1

I REMEMBER THE FIRST TIME I saw the animated movie *The Pilgrim's Progress*. At the beginning of the film, we see the main character, Christian, carrying a pack on his back. Throughout his journey, this pack slowly grows heavier as he finds his way to Christ. During the scene where Christian climbs to the cross, I cry every time. Why? Because it depicts something that we all experience: carrying a burden that others often don't see and how that burden gets heavier and heavier the longer we try to carry it alone.

One of the most frequent prayer requests I receive from friends around the world is for depression. Although I don't understand what it is like to struggle with depression, I do understand that it's very real. I think we all need to understand how real it is and how real the devil is who wants to capitalize on it for our destruction. He would love nothing more than for depression (or any other mental health issue—he's not picky) to sideline us. But I don't want to stand for that. Not for myself, not for my family and friends, and not for you.

What I do know is that when someone is facing a battle, including depression, it seems often no one knows about it till it's become a massive struggle. It's like Christian's backpack. Slowly growing heavier the longer he journeys. Why is that? Several friends have told me it's because we don't want to be a bother when we're going through something hard. Other people seem to be doing just fine in life, maybe even thriving. So why burden them with our struggles? And that is exactly the lie the devil wants us to believe. Here's the truth: Galatians 6:2 tells us, "Share each other's burdens, and in this way obey the law of Christ." Oof! You know what this means, right? That whether we are the one in a season of struggling or we are able to lend support to someone who is, God gives us compassion and mercy. Sharing burdens (especially a mental health issue like depression) can be so vulnerable and just plain hard to do. But what a good God we serve. Even when we hold back or make a mistake or a misstep, He's right there, ready to catch us and put faithful friends around us who will help ease our load. And these faithful friends can also help share God's truth with us when it's too hard to see for ourselves.

As a friend, I also want to share some "God truths" (personalized versions of Scripture verses) that we can speak and pray over ourselves. Many of these come from the Psalms and were written by King David, who experienced much anguish in his life. Yet he had one good thing going for him: he kept turning back to the Lord as his source of strength, knowing God could pull him out of any pit.

Feel free to say these out loud, pray on them, or even write them down and work on memorizing them because the more they are in our hearts, the more easily we can declare God's Word over any situation.

Deuteronomy 31:8: God will never leave me. He goes before me!

2 Samuel 22:29: God is my lamp and lights my darkness!

Psalm 9:9-10: The Lord is my stronghold, and I put my trust in Him!

Psalm 34:17: God hears my voice when I cry for help and delivers me from my troubles!

Psalm 40:1-3: God heard me, pulled me out of the pit of destruction, and He makes my steps secure!

Psalm 42:11: God is my hope!

Psalm 94:19: God cheers my soul!

Jeremiah 17:7-8: God is where I put my trust, and He will plant my roots in Him!

The thing about depression is this: no matter where it comes from or how it manifests, its aim is to keep us holed up. There are many steps we need to take to counteract depression, but as believers, all of us can repeat God's Word to ourselves and to our friends who are struggling. This may not be *all* we need, but it's a great start to help build up our spirits. We can activate faith on each other's behalf when the fight seems too much to bear.

Our God is a God of order, and there is a right order in which to do things. When it comes to our burdens, we need to first invite God in. That's straight from God's Word. Psalm 55:22 says, "Give your burdens to the LORD, and he will take care of you. He will not permit the godly to slip and fall." God loves an invitation—He's all about them! When I've faced struggles that don't seem to lift or resolve, I've eventually realized that I hadn't even invited the Lord into the situation, asked for His help, or made room to hear His voice. Let's not be stubborn about needing the Lord.

Once we have invited the Lord into our need, we must take action. We might not feel like doing anything, but we have to fight that tendency. Let's saturate our souls with God's truth so that when the pit of depression rears its head and tries to take another day from us, we know what to do. And let's not forget to praise God. In faith, let's declare what we know to be true. I know our faith may feel weak, but we can still speak of God's promises, knowing that even when our words fall short, His faithfulness won't!

Let's walk forward into this week asking the Lord into the feelings of despair we face, knowing that whether they have been around a short time or we've been battling them for years, God will fight them head-on for and with us.

Pray

Dear Lord, You meet me in the middle of my struggles and the toll they take. You can walk with me. You *do* walk with me. This week, I pray that something or someone would come alongside me and encourage me in my challenges. You are God over every part of my life. You see. You know. You value even when I am walking through hard, hard things. Would You give me wisdom on how to counteract the lies of the enemy? Would You also give me peace each day as I navigate the season I'm in that weighs heavy on me? I speak Your name, Jesus, over my fear, my anxiety, my depression, and anything else I face. I invite You to be Lord over every area of my life, even the ones I try to keep to myself. I know Your name is a conquering name. And I want to be a conqueror through You. In Jesus' name, amen.

There is nothing more solid than God's Word!

7

Hidden in Our Hearts

I have hidden your word in my heart, that I might not sin against you.
I praise you, O Lord; teach me your decrees.
I have recited aloud all the regulations you have given us.
I have rejoiced in your laws as much as in riches.
I will study your commandments and reflect on your ways.
I will delight in your decrees and not forget your word.

PSALM 119:11-16

MY DAD ISN'T MUCH OF A READER. He would tell you that. Yet if you looked at his Bible, you would see pages weathered from being read over and over. You would see asterisks and highlights and dots from where he has marked his place year after year of reading through the Bible. Some years, my dad even reads through it twice—even though he "isn't much of a reader."

My mom, on the other hand, is a voracious reader. She could stay up until 2 a.m. reading a book she just can't put down. But she too would tell you that of all the books she has read, the Bible is the one she has read the most.

One childhood memory I treasure is seeing my dad reading his Bible every morning and watching my mom study her Bible alongside her various devotionals. To this day, she still has a basket next to her chair with various Bible translations and devos that she is working through. You know what I appreciate about my parents? Although they had different approaches to reading the Bible, they both *did* it! And still do. Generational impact right there. I want to have the same impact on my children, although sometimes I feel like I'm really lagging. Maybe you have felt that way too—not just about reading the Bible but about really learning and knowing it.

You find a new reading plan, you have good intentions, and then March hits and, while you should be on day sixty, you are still trudging through day forty. Before you know it, the distance between where you should be and where you are seems to grow as wide as the Grand Canyon. I tend to get so caught up in staying caught up that I find myself in one of two places: giving up or just plowing through to finish instead of reading with a purpose. But I'm trying, and I don't ever want to lose my zest for deep-diving to learn more about God.

Another thing that stands out to me about my parents is their ability to recite Scripture. Truthfully? It still blows me away. Because it means they aren't just reading to flip pages and check boxes—they have always been reading the Bible with a purpose. It's the same purpose we should all be reading with: to live out Psalm 119:11, which says, "I have hidden your word in my heart, that I might not sin against you." Let's back up to verse 7, which says, "As I learn your righteous regulations, I will thank you by living as I should!" and verse 9, "How can a young person stay pure? By obeying your word." Then verse 15 says, "I will study your commandments and reflect on your ways." So many verses point to *reading* God's Word and *knowing* God's Word. Why is this so important?

Because when a moment comes in our life that shakes the ground beneath us, we need something solid to stand on. And there is nothing more solid than God's Word! No relationship, no job, nothing else is going to give you the foundation that God's Word provides. I was just telling my boys the other day that the Bible is the only book that has continued to stand the test of time, hold up to historical analysis, and constantly sell all over the world. Unlike our feelings and opinions, God's truth doesn't change. Ever. The author of any other book could change their mind about what they wrote and walk a different path. But God doesn't do that. "The LORD's plans stand firm forever; his intentions can never be shaken" (Psalm 33:11).

So why memorize? Why not just read? Because when those tough moments come, God's Word hidden in our heart becomes a way to *pray*, *praise*, and *put up a fight* against the ways of the devil. We can battle the devil's lies with God's truth. We can sing praise the same way David did in his distress. And we can call out the promises of God and claim them for our own as His children as long as we are living in obedience to Him. When we allow Jesus to be Lord over our life, we receive a new type of freedom that we can use to fight our battles, knowing that God is fighting for us as well!

A quick tip on how to start memorizing Scripture: I'm sure we all sing songs and know certain lyrics like the back of our hand. So use repetition to your advantage. Start small and memorize Scripture passages in chunks. Repeat them often. Turn them into songs. I like to put motions to the words too. Memorize with your kids. This keeps me accountable because kids want to learn! My dad likes to write a verse on a note card and keep it in his car as he memorizes. Whatever works for you, do it!

Let's walk forward into this week and choose not only to keep going in our Bible reading but to memorize one verse and hide it in our hearts through these next seven days. As Proverbs 3:1 says, "My child, never forget the things I have taught you. Store my commands in your heart." Once you memorize one verse, you'll do another, and before you know it, you'll be a memorizing machine!

Pray

Dear Lord, thank You that You've given me Your Word, the Truth, to guide me every day. The Bible helps me to know You more as my heavenly Father, Savior, and Advocate. I pray that You would help me be disciplined not just to read my Bible but to know You more deeply and fully. Thank You that by memorizing Scripture I can tuck Your truths in my heart and store them to build up and encourage my faith anytime I need it. Because the Bible is living and active, I can rely on what it says for anything I walk through in life. Give me the discipline and the wisdom to put You first every day in all I do. In Jesus' name, amen.

God's vision for our lives is so much better than our own.

8

New Vision

"For I know the plans I have for you," says the LORD. "They are plans for good and not for disaster, to give you a future and a hope. In those days when you pray, I will listen. If you look for me wholeheartedly, you will find me."

JEREMIAH 29:11-13

THIS DAY WAS YEARS IN THE MAKING. Like seven or eight years. I was probably turning thirty when I first desired to get surgery to correct my vision. I had been wearing glasses since I was nine and contacts since I was twelve, so I was used to my bad vision, but I was nearly half-blind without aid. When I heard about the possibility of laser eye surgery, I quickly began my research—which ended just as quickly when I found out that you can't be pregnant or nursing (or within six months of either) to be eligible. We were happily in the middle of our childbearing years, so I put that idea on the back burner.

I waited patiently for when I could explore the possibility again. When I turned thirty-seven and a year had passed since our seventh child, Lucy, was born, I got examined again. Turns out the path to unaided great vision wouldn't be as easy as I thought because my corneas are so thin. Who knew? I didn't qualify for LASIK, the easier version of eye surgery. And I barely qualified for the alternative. As the doctors explained that alternative procedure and all the difficulties I would face in recovery, I thought to myself that they must not like making money because they were pretty good at convincing me my eyesight may be better left alone.

I went home unsure if the result I longed for would be worth the pain. My surgery was scheduled for three months out. Let me tell you, for those three months, I struggled! I went back and forth on all the pros and cons, and I almost canceled the procedure. The two days leading up to the surgery, despite all the research I had done, I felt such intense fear about the procedure, the pain that would likely follow, and the uncertainty of success. The fear gripped me to the point of tears. I even wondered, *Lord, is this You showing me that this isn't the right decision?* But when I prayed, I realized that if I had qualified for LASIK, I would have done it in a heartbeat. I was experiencing fear of unknown pain, not fear of the surgery itself.

Fast-forward to surgery day, and I felt such a peace in that waiting room. The surgery took all of three minutes (and it was a fascinating experience). From there, it was just me and a few days of complete darkness and rest. As I was recovering from surgery and lying in the dark room to rest my eyes, I felt like the Lord spoke something so challenging to me but in such an encouraging, gentle way. Some of us have been going along in life with the same lenses for a long time, viewing the world with the same perspective. Maybe that's you. I know it's been me in various seasons. Early in my marriage, I got stuck in a rut of viewing only the negative parts of my husband. It was like I went into autopilot mode—only seeing things one way and not considering that maybe there was another way. Or I became comfortable with how I saw things because it kept my life comfortable, and I'd rather not be challenged to change. (Because we all know that being challenged often changes us—eek! That's not always fun, is it?)

But here's the thing. God wants to give us new sight—*His* sight. New vision—*His* vision. He wants us to view the world through the lens of His love, His order, and His plans (not to mention His boundaries, His freedom, and His forgiveness)! First Corinthians 13:12 says, "Now we see things imperfectly, like puzzling reflections in a mirror, but then we will see everything with perfect clarity. All that I know now is partial and incomplete, but then I will know everything completely, just as God now knows me completely."

Choosing that—intentionally choosing change—can be scary, right? It can be uncomfortable. Actually, it *will* be uncomfortable. So why would we put ourselves through that kind of pain? Because God's vision for our lives is *so* much better than our own. I like that word *completely* at the end of 1 Corinthians 13:12. With God in control of our lives, we will never see the same way again. We will see *completely* when we rely on Him. Instead of putting on our rose-colored glasses each morning, we begin to see with clarity. Instead of looking to social media or people's opinions, we look to the Word of God, knowing it speaks truth and gives us a heavenly perspective on how to live. And we don't even need to go through surgery to get there. We just need to be willing to say, "God, give me Your eyes for my life, my family, my job, my relationships, this world! Help me to see like You see and turn my eyes to the things that matter most!" Sure, it might be uncomfortable for a while. But discomfort is temporary compared to what God has for us in this life and in eternity.

Want to know something so cool and so like God? The day of the surgery, I felt nothing but peace. My whole spirit was at peace as I walked through each step of the procedure. It was a peace I couldn't come up with on my own, and I knew the Lord had settled my spirit. I believe He will do the same for you—for all of us—as we let go of our self-centered perspectives and exchange them for the vision God has set for each of us. I know that's hard. I know fear creeps in. But we can practice trusting in God for *His* perspective. Sometimes in the beginning this just means repeating the words of Scripture even when we don't believe them. Over time, what we practice begins to settle into our hearts and soon becomes part of us. Before you know it, we aren't just repeating words; we are speaking them out with confidence and faith that the Lord will do what He said He would do!

Let's walk forward into this week asking the Lord to show us any areas where we aren't seeing in the way He wants us to see. Then let's take it one step further and ask the Lord to help our vision change so we can see the way He does.

Pray

Dear Lord, sometimes it is so hard to step outside my own perspective. But you see a bigger picture than I do, and You know me better than I know myself. I don't want to be robbed of the joy, the goodness, or the bigness of the plans You have for me just because I'm unwilling to change or see things differently. Help me take my eyes off myself and my wants and turn them to You. Give me new vision and clarity for the path You have planned for me. You direct my steps, and I want to make room for Your direction. Forgive me for times I've tried to force things that aren't of You, Lord, instead of letting You lead. Thank You for Your good plans ahead. Lord, I ask that this week would be a restart, and even if it's a little uncomfortable, please help me trust You in the process. In Jesus' name, amen.

We are created with purpose, developing and blooming from the inside out, pruned and nurtured with great intention by the One who cares about us the most.

9

From the Inside Out

The LORD said to Samuel, "Don't judge by his appearance or height, for I have rejected him. The LORD doesn't see things the way you see them. People judge by outward appearance, but the LORD looks at the heart."

1 SAMUEL 16:7

THE MOST RANDOM THING I searched for online the other day was "How do figs form?" I didn't want to believe what I'd heard about the process because it kind of ruined the whole experience for me. You see, I love fruit. Love it! Have my whole life. And figs are one fruit I really enjoy, though they can be hard to find. I often convince people to try figs, though they are usually let down by the flavor. But not me (and not my kids). We all love them. But they have to be fresh! None of this Fig Newtons stuff. That doesn't even compare.

Back to the story. When someone told me how figs grow, I had to look it up for myself. What I found confirmed what I'd been told: as a fig forms, a certain type of wasp crawls inside to pollinate it, losing its wings because the opening is so small. The wasp lays eggs and dies inside the fig and eventually disintegrates into protein for the fruit. You can imagine my distaste. I wasn't sure if I ever wanted to eat a fig again (just like you might not be sure how this week's devotional will be anywhere near encouraging with the picture I just painted!). Spoiler alert: I still eat figs, and this devo will, in fact, encourage you. And heads up—I'm going to show you how we are similar to both the fig and the process by which it forms.

Did you know that figs grow from the inside out? You never see the flowers. But they are there—changing, growing, blooming, and forming into the fig we pick, all protected by the outer layer. During that process, the eggs laid by the female wasp hatch, and the young wasps take pollen from that fig's flowers, crawl out, and find another fig tree to complete the same pollination process. And now that I've officially convinced you to never try figs (that leaves more for me, I guess), let me convince you of this.

Giving our lives to Jesus is similar to the process of fig development. We go around in life looking for something to bring joy. We meet Jesus. We come into His presence, and sometimes that process of coming to Jesus means a few things get clipped or cut along the way. Although that may hurt a little, we don't need those things weighing us down or holding us back from living fully in His presence. We present ourselves to Him vulnerable, a bit broken and bare. We feed off His goodness for a while to gain strength, and our new self is built up in Christ. The more we grow in Him, the more our old self dies. (Look up Ephesians 4:22-24 to see what the Bible says about this process.) But that's not the end. What becomes of us? Something new! Something beautiful and delightful and prized and treasured in the hand of the beholder. A fruit that is esteemed and precious.

Did you know that figs are mentioned in the Bible twenty-five times? In Deuteronomy, Moses listed fig trees as one of the things the Israelites would gain in the Promised Land (see Deuteronomy 8:8). Figs were right up there with pomegranates, olive oil, and honey. They were considered to have a richness and decadence about them: the deep colors, the gentle smell and taste, the unique shape. Nurturing figs requires much skill and care, so a healthy, mature fig tree is the sign of a faithful gardener.

Whether you eat figs or not, all of us bear resemblance to how this fruit forms: we are created with purpose, developing and blooming from the inside out, pruned and nurtured with great intention by the One who cares about us the most—God, our Master Gardener. He faithfully tends to us with unmatched gentleness, keeps us growing year after year, and deepens our roots in Him. Then we can blossom in humility, knowing that our hearts are protected by God's covering.

Let's walk forward into this week confident that even when things on the outside might not look like a beautiful fruit, the real work is happening where it needs to: inside our hearts. And that the same God who cares for the fig and the wasp that pollinates it cares even more about growing you into who you are meant to be. Now go try a fresh fig if you can find one!

Pray

Dear Lord, I want to grow how You designed me to grow: from the inside out. I want my heart toward You to matter more than anything else, and I want my roots to run deep and not shallow. I want to be pruned even if it hurts a little so You can grow me into someone new, into the person You want me to be. Help me to recognize the things that matter in Your eyes and to focus on those. And just like the fig is growing before anyone can see the beauty of the inside, help me to see the beauty in the process and not just the end result. God, You are so gracious to tend to me in every season and nurture the areas of my life that need growth. Thank You for Your faithfulness, and I ask that You continue to help me bloom big so that when others see me, they see You. In Jesus' name, amen.

Ask the Lord to help you, equip you, and go with you.

10

Strong and Courageous

"This is my command—be strong and courageous! Do not be afraid or discouraged. For the LORD your God is with you wherever you go."

JOSHUA 1:9

I WAS IN THE MIDDLE OF LISTENING to the books of Deuteronomy and Joshua on audio when I had to pause, go back, and count how many times the Lord said the same thing to Joshua. Because when God says something repeatedly, we probably better listen and understand why. Between Deuteronomy chapter 31 and Joshua chapter 1, the words "Be strong and courageous" are repeated seven times. Seven times in five chapters.

When I think of "strong and courageous," especially in the Bible, I always imagine some warrior-type leader who is a head taller than the rest and pretty athletic. Anyone else? I mean, makes sense for someone who is a leader among a massive group of people. Why, then, would someone like that need a reminder to be strong and courageous? Because no matter who you are or what you are capable of, we all need someone reminding us of our purpose and cheering us on to do it well. Especially when a lot is at stake, you know, like going off to conquer cities. Just everyday happenings, right?

But I want to take you back a couple pages to the book of Numbers, when the Israelites had just left Egypt and were near the Promised Land. Moses sent twelve spies to check out the land and report back. Ten came back panicked and got everyone else in a panic too. But two of the spies saw it differently (see Numbers 13:25-33). They saw the Promised Land through strong and courageous eyes. They saw what God had promised while everyone else panicked.

Can you guess who one of them was? That's right—our guy Joshua. Along with the other brave spy, Caleb, he said, "Do not rebel against the Lord, and don't be afraid of the people of the land. . . . They have no protection, but the Lord is with us! Don't be afraid of them!" (Numbers 14:9). When everyone else forgets about God's promises, Joshua remembers, and it gives him strength and courage. Because of this, he ends up becoming the leader of the Israelites when Moses dies.

Do you know what's interesting about strength and courage? They are actually two very different things. On their own, neither will take you as far as you'd like, but when put together, they are a force. I don't think it's an accident that the Lord kept them together in his reminders to Joshua. By definition, strength is to exert or resist force while courage is more of a mental perseverance. You can see why one needs the other. Strength may help you knock down a few bricks and launch yourself over some cool obstacles, but courage is what's going to get you to the end of the course when your muscles are tanked. Joshua needed both. We need both. And God knows that! So He gives us reminders (and sometimes a lot of them if needed).

God is such a good and faithful God, isn't He? I'm so thankful that the Holy Spirit speaks to us daily and reminds us of what we need to hear (that is, when we allow Him to speak into our lives). I'm also thankful we have the Word of God to look to for reminders. When we are rooted in God's Word and consuming it consistently, it opens the door for the Holy Spirit to minister to us exactly how we need. In fact, the Spirit speaks to us most frequently through God's Word! Which makes it all the more exciting to read our Bibles and deepen our relationship with God.

Maybe you aren't conquering cities like Joshua. But maybe you are planning to move—to uproot your family and plant yourselves somewhere else. Maybe you aren't facing a massive army or giants that are twice your size. But maybe you are facing a tough diagnosis that feels like a giant. Maybe you aren't the leader of a huge community that is complaining about your every decision. But maybe you are a leader trying to act with integrity in your own sphere of influence, yet you feel all alone. Your circumstances aren't exactly like Joshua's, but my guess is you have a lot more in common with him than you think.

We need the same reminders today that Joshua needed back then. We need the same faithful God whom Joshua needed then as he led the Israelites. We need the same whispers, sometimes repeated over and over to build us up and equip us for whatever we may be facing. We need to be people who are strong and courageous and count on the Lord to help fight every single one of our battles. You with me? Say yes!

When God told Joshua to be strong and courageous in Joshua 1:9, He prefaced it by also saying, "This is my command." So I'm not encouraging you in this just because it sounds good and pumps you up (although I'm doing that too). I'm sharing it because it's God's command that we all need. And when he puts forth a command that's for my benefit, I want to follow it the best I can. I know you do too.

Let's walk forward into this week reminded that, whatever you are facing, you can be strong and courageous. The caveat is this: don't try to do it on your own. Ask the Lord to help you, equip you, and go with you in whatever you are facing this week. When you ask, He will do it because He loves when we follow His commands.

Pray

Dear Lord, You are faithful and consistent even when I'm not. Thank You that no matter what circumstance I'm facing and no matter what season I'm in, You show up. And You don't just show up—You encourage me and remind me to be strong and courageous *in You*! As I learn to pour my life into Your hands, Lord, You pour back into me the grace I need to face what's ahead. I pray that my default would be to give everything to You first, knowing that You will give me the extra measure I need. You are in it all, Lord. Thank You that You see a bigger picture than I do and that, even when I panic at what is in front of or around me, life doesn't surprise You. Lord, I want to be strong and courageous for You. Help me to walk forward with increased confidence and boldness, knowing that You have already won the battles on my behalf. In Jesus' name, amen.

The Lord sees us loving others, and He will bless our efforts.

11

Cheerleader

Let us think of ways to motivate one another to acts of love and good works. And let us not neglect our meeting together, as some people do, but encourage one another, especially now that the day of his return is drawing near.

HEBREWS 10:24-25

I WISH YOU COULD HAVE KNOWN my great-aunt Phyllis. Our kids all called her "Double-Great-Aunt Phyllis," and she laughed every time she heard that name. She was my mom's aunt, and she died at the rich age of ninety-four. She loved the Lord the entire second half of her life. She never married and was never well-to-do by the standards of the world, yet when you met her you knew that her cup was fuller than most. Overflowing, in fact. One of my favorite memories of Aunt Phyllis is when I was a young girl playing sports. If we played anywhere near her town, she was there! She sat through summer heat and fall winds to watch us play our various games. But what she loved most was baseball. As she sat there wearing her glasses with the clip-on shades and her baseball hat over her short white hair, she would cheer us on nonstop. Her voice was the loudest in the crowd. But the best part? If she happened to say a cheer before a good thing happened, she repeated that exact cheer the *entire* rest of the game, convinced that was "the thing" that would keep the streak going.

My entire memory of Aunt Phyllis is defined by how she would cheer others on. It didn't matter if I was playing sports, studying to be a nurse, umpiring a softball game, competing for a scholarship on stage, or playing piano at a recital—she was the biggest cheerleader. But you know what she cheered us on in the most? Loving the Lord. Even to her last days, when she couldn't remember much, she remembered Scripture. She would repeat it, mumble it, sing it, pray it. She would look at us all with her glazed blue eyes and shrug her shoulders like she didn't know it was happening. And through her songs and prayers and holding of our hands, she continued to cheer us on.

In our current culture, we lack good cheerleaders. And I don't just mean the kind at sports games. I mean the kind who come alongside you and genuinely cheer on what the Lord is doing in your life (and help you discern the things that don't matter as much). You know the ones. They are few and far between, it seems. Do you feel like you only have one or two? That's okay! It's more of a quality over quantity thing. And if you don't have anyone cheering you on right now, here's my encouragement: First, know that the same God who created the galaxies and planets is the God who cheers you on. Second, choose to be other people's cheerleader. Do it with a genuine heart. Affirm the ways the Lord is at work in their lives, bearing good fruit. Show up for them.

It's easy to yearn for something, but it's an entirely different thing to say, "Ya know what? I may not have that for me right now, but I sure can be that for other people." What a perspective shift—but a hard one for sure. The beautiful part of this attitude is that the Lord sees us loving others, and I believe, in His good timing, He will bless our efforts. I believe that because I've seen it—not only in the life of Double-Great-Aunt Phyllis but in others too. Aunt Phyllis had no children of her own. But she had a family of her own. In us. In all her nieces and nephews whom she purposely invested in. Because of her investment of time and encouragement, she created a legacy that I can promise you didn't die with her. At her funeral, the repeated theme from those who shared was that she cheered them on: in their motherhood, in their emptiness, in their sorrow, in their joy, in their marriage, in their pastoring, in their leading, in their jobs. But most of all, in their walk with the Lord. One of the things I see in my own mom is that cheerleader spirit that Aunt Phyllis passed to her. Legacy.

I want to carry that legacy in my own life. I want to be a person who chooses to cheer instead of jeer when someone accomplishes something that the Lord put before them. When my friends succeed, I want to be the first to call and say, "I'm so proud of you. You did so well, and you impacted so many people." I want them to know that they have someone in their corner who will cheer on the good—and pray and share wisdom in areas that might not be fruitful. Because that's also what a true cheerleader does. They pray for and give godly counsel to those they care about most.

Let's walk forward into this week and find one way to cheer someone on. Write an encouraging card to a mom in the middle of raising little ones or text someone and tell them how proud you are of them—or better yet, tell them face-to-face when you see them. Being a cheerleader in someone's life might not seem like a big deal, but it can leave a lifelong imprint on their heart!

Pray

Dear Lord, thank You so much that I have the opportunity to cheer others on. I want to be an encourager, Lord, and I want to do it in a genuine way that shows I care. Help me find ways to uniquely show up for the people in my life. Most of all, Lord, help me to encourage and cheer them on in their walk with You. And thank You, Lord, that You are my encourager. That You walk right alongside me. Help me to leave a legacy that includes You as the foundation of all I do. Give me wisdom on how to see people the way You do, and help me to be like Double-Great-Aunt Phyllis and love the people You put around us. In Jesus' name, amen.

We can choose to respond in peace to value others instead of always aiming to be right or win an argument.

12

Practice Peace

Do all that you can to live in peace with everyone.

ROMANS 12:18

YOU KNOW WHAT'S HARD? Relationships. People. You and me. Whether friendships, marriages, parents, siblings, distant relatives, or coworkers, it seems that there is always a situation that is difficult or sticky to navigate. We struggle to know whether we should let things go or face them head-on, undercommunicate or overcommunicate, tell them how we feel or keep it to ourselves, and so on. So many options—sometimes too many options.

I remember sitting in our kitchen one night as Tim and I vented about a relational situation with my parents but tried to do it in an honoring way. When Tim and I navigate relationships with people who bug us, we try to remind each other, "There are lots of things about us that bug other people." That night we laid it all out in front of my parents and asked, "What do you think?"

My parents acknowledged that our frustration was valid while agreeing that we all have traits that don't mesh well with everyone. I appreciate that my parents tend to see the whole picture even when all they hear is our side. We asked them what we should do. Should we talk it out with the other party? And that's when my dad mentioned Romans 12:18: "Do all that you can to live in peace with everyone."

Does that really mean *everyone*? Surely God knows there are some people who just make that too difficult. Surely He knows when we have exhausted all resources to make a challenging relationship work. Because surely God wouldn't ask us to choose peace over setting someone straight and telling our side of the story.

Well, yes, He would, which means we have to trust that God really meant what He said in Romans 12:18.

I remember a conversation I had with two of my boys a while back when they weren't getting along. Neither of them wanted to let the issue go and move on. I can relate. Can you? So I asked them a few questions: "Will this matter tomorrow? Will you remember it in a week? When you get to heaven and ask Jesus what really mattered, will this be His answer?" I could tell by their small smiles that they understood the point of these questions. I don't remember a single time when holding a grudge or reliving an argument over and over helped me. When I choose peace instead of proving my point, I look back and think, *Wow, it's been a while since we've had an argument. That feels great.*

Does this mean we should never disagree, question things, or start conversations about difficult topics? No! But we need discernment from the Lord and wisdom for how to handle any given situation. The Holy Spirit will certainly be faithful to nudge us in the right direction.

If you are struggling with family dynamics, marriage communication, friendship difficulties, or other relational challenges, you aren't alone. But you also aren't stuck there. We can control what we can control. I think I've said that at least a few hundred times in our house. The best part is this means we can choose to pursue peace in our relationships. Don't be fooled by the devil, who aims to "steal and kill and destroy" through divisiveness (John 10:10). He'd love nothing more than to see your relationships dissolve and everyone suffer. But don't give in. I believe we can choose to respond in peace to value others instead of always aiming to be right or win an argument. Even if we feel like we've lost, we really haven't. Because a week later, my bet is we won't even remember the issue. Or if we do, we will be able to see how the Lord fought our battles for us when we didn't take them into our own hands.

Let's walk forward into this week knowing that when we find ourselves in the middle of a relational exchange that's on the verge of escalating (or one that frustrates us to no end), we can repeat Romans 12:18 in our heads and ask God to help us do it. The more we practice peace even when we don't feel like it, the more it will become part of our natural response. When peace becomes part of who we are because God is actively working in our hearts, that is better than winning any argument!

Pray

Dear Lord, guard my heart and mind and cover my mouth so I won't dishonor You or others with my words. Protect my mind and give me wisdom to speak life even when it's uncomfortable and hard. To give grace even when I feel others deserve the opposite. To aim to live in peace with those around me. I want to choose peace in my own life, but I know I can't do that without Your help. Would You work in my heart to make it more like Yours? I want a heart that loves people and doesn't hold on to grudges or carry offense even if I've been wronged. I pray against the spirit of divisiveness and anger and short tempers. And I pray for life-giving conversations and healing in my difficult relationships. I pray for moments where I walk away thinking, *Wow, I wasn't expecting that—but God!* You are the One who created relationships, Lord, so I give all of mine to You and ask You to help me honor You in every single one. In Jesus' name, amen.

If God prioritized rest, how much more should we do the same?

13

Rest in the Lord

Come to me, all of you who are weary and carry heavy burdens, and I will give you rest. Take my yoke upon you. Let me teach you, because I am humble and gentle at heart, and you will find rest for your souls. For my yoke is easy to bear, and the burden I give you is light.

MATTHEW 11:28–30

THERE WAS A DAY A WHILE BACK when one of my kids was falling apart. Mentally, emotionally, physically—it was just a tough day all around. I could hear it in his voice and see it in his body language. We'd had a couple weeks with full schedules and not a lot of downtime, and it showed. So I strongly suggested (mandated) that he go lie down on his bed and take a short rest. He sobbed as he headed back to the bedroom. Shoulders slumped and dripping tears, he said, "I don't need a rest, though." I tried to hold back my chuckle. All of his body language was shouting, "Let me lie down!" As an adult, I wish I could explain to him that rests are, in fact, *wonderful*! But kids don't ever want to miss out on fun, and in their minds that is what resting means. Which is why, when I tell my littlest boy he's taking a nap, he says, "Is everyone else taking a nap?" He's just making certain he won't miss out on anything important.

Like my kids, sometimes I forgo rest because I don't want to miss what's happening. Sound familiar? All of us compromise on rest, whether to do something fun or to catch up on work. Guess who eventually suffers the most? We do. Our bodies, minds, attitudes, and decision-making skills are all affected by lack of rest. There's nothing wrong with working hard—in fact, hard work is biblical. Proverbs 21:5 says, "Good planning and hard work lead to prosperity, but hasty shortcuts lead to poverty." But you know what else is biblical? Rest. In fact, it's a command.

From the beginning of time, God marked rest as an important and necessary part of life. God Himself rested on the seventh day of Creation (see Genesis 2:2). Then He went even further and declared the seventh day of the week holy, and He blessed that day (see Genesis 2:3). The One who created the entire universe and holds it in the palm of His hand . . . that God chose to rest from His work. And if He prioritized rest, how much more should we do the same? God made our bodies, and he knows they can't function properly without rest. He built a rhythm of waking and sleeping into our bodies and our world.

Yet even knowing all this, we tend to fight rest. We stay up late just to finish "one more thing" because if we don't, our to-do list won't get any shorter or we won't have any time to ourselves.

Trust me when I say that, as a mom, I know how hard it is to go rest. I mean, I can't just stop in the middle of the day and say, "Well, kids, it's Mommy's rest time . . . see you in an hour." But we *can* find ways to rest in the Lord that don't always include falling asleep for a power nap each day. Rest can mean many things.

There are a few ways we can rest *and* rest in the Lord. By that I mean we can allow ourselves to be at peace with what the Lord has for us and allow the Lord to minister to us in that peace. Some of the practical ways we can do this include: sleep, worship, prayer, saying no to things we don't have the capacity for, managing our time well, putting the Lord first in our days instead of last, taking time to listen for His voice, and setting aside times of quiet (I know this is hard with little ones). This isn't an exhaustive list by any means, but it's a start. And sometimes that's what we need: a place to start and an encouragement to be a bit more intentional about something God meant for our good and for our health.

Want to know something interesting? When we intentionally choose *not* to rest, we are disobeying God's commands according to Hebrews 4:9-11: "There remains, then, a Sabbath-rest for the people of God; for anyone who enters God's rest also rests from their works, just as God did from his. Let us, therefore, make every effort to enter that rest, so that no one will perish by following their example of disobedience" (NIV). Rest is obedience. Rest is a good gift from

God, one He purposefully designed. When I don't choose it or I don't make it a consistent habit in my life, I get all out of sorts: first my attitude and how I respond to people, then exhaustion from being overwhelmed in every area, usually followed by a complete mental (and sometimes physical) collapse. Nothing good comes from lack of rest.

Let's walk forward into this week encouraged to find a moment in our day(s) to rest. Pick a day, pick a time, and stick to it. Even if it's just five minutes of sitting down and praying or listening to worship music with our eyes closed (that's a great start), my guess is it will do more for us than we realize. It will refresh us and help us see that rest doesn't take away from our lives—in fact, it restores us to keep going and, better yet, helps us realize the pace the Lord wants us to move.

Pray

Dear Lord, please help me to be aware of when I need to yield to rest versus getting everything done. Help me to realize that rest does not equal laziness. Lord, I want my life to honor You, and that includes doing the things that You've commanded. I know that You will provide rest that restores and refreshes my body and mind. Father, some seasons can be wearier than others. Build me up and give me strength and a renewed sense for the next season. Let me lean into the rest You give and the rest You call me to. In Jesus' name, amen.

I don't want to be so stuck in my comfort zone that I miss the things God has for me that might change my life forever.

14

Forward in Faith

When you go through deep waters, I will be with you. When you go through rivers of difficulty, you will not drown. When you walk through the fire of oppression, you will not be burned up; the flames will not consume you.

ISAIAH 43:2

I LOVE THE OCEAN, but I also have a healthy fear of it. It's something about not being able to see to the bottom, coupled with the fact that I watched the movie *Jaws* once—that was enough for me to keep a safe distance! Yet I'll still go out and snorkel in the areas where the bottom isn't too far out of sight. Tim, on the other hand, loves the ocean and is pretty fearless. He will swim out into deep waters so he can see things no one else gets to see. When he tells me all he saw, part of me oohs and ahhs at the thought of being brave enough to jump in fearlessly. Yet I still find myself staying close to shore.

Have you ever heard the song that says, "You call me out upon the waters, the great unknown where feet may fail"?[1] I can relate to that feeling. Our homes and the spaces we create for ourselves are much more comfortable than trying something new God is calling us to and possibly hating it—or, even worse, failing at whatever we are trying. So we stay in the familiar and don't walk too far outside of our comfort zones because it could be terrible. But what if it's not?

There's this guy in the Bible, named Nehemiah, who worked for the Persian king as his cup-bearer. This position may sound lowly, but it was actually very significant. The cup-bearer was known to be one of the most trustworthy people because he was responsible for serving beverages to the king and making sure

[1] Matt Crocker, Joel Houston, and Salomon Lightelm, "Oceans (Where Feet May Fail)," on *Zion*, performed by Hillsong UNITED and TAYA, Hillsong UNITED, 2013.

he had the drinks he needed. So safe to say, Nehemiah was a stand-up guy who lived a pretty comfortable life. Until that all changed.

Nehemiah found out that Jerusalem, the city of his ancestors, was in ruins. Burned up. And he wanted to rebuild it. So first he prayed and called out to God, and then he asked the king to let him go (see Nehemiah 1:4-11; 2:5). You can imagine how this might affect a king—letting one of his most trusted people leave. But the king agreed that Nehemiah could go to Jerusalem. Not only that, but the king sent letters with Nehemiah so he would find favor during his mission.

Nehemiah chose the uncomfortable and unknown over the comfortable and known. He had no clue what he was getting into. But he knew who would go before him: God!

When Nehemiah arrived in Jerusalem, things were worse than he'd thought. Although many people had come to help, some showed great opposition. Isn't that typical? The Lord plants something in our hearts and asks us to step outside of our comfort zone to accomplish what He has asked of us. We agree, thinking God will make the way easy. *Wrong!* Stepping into God's calling doesn't equal easy. But His wisdom guides us (if we listen), and His understanding keeps us on the right path.

The devil will use every trick in his bag to get us to question ourselves and our purpose. The thing is, he has very few tricks. But what the enemy knows is that repetition wears a person down. So he makes us question what God really said. Then he puts people in our way to try to block our path. And if all that fails, he uses fear to deter us from completing what God put in our heart. The enemy knows that if we complete what God sets for us to do, the Kingdom impact will be further reaching than we can imagine. And Kingdom growing means devil shrinking. Amen!

When we don't see what God's up to but we choose to obey and step out of our comfort zone anyway, the result is far greater than we could imagine. What I love about Nehemiah is that, even when opposition came, his very first reply was, "The God of heaven will help us succeed" (Nehemiah 2:20). What a guy! I want to be like Nehemiah. Hearing from the Lord, acting on what He has called me to do, and facing it without fear, knowing that what God started, no one can stop.

For our tenth anniversary, Tim and I visited an island in Hawaii that we had never been to before. I was sixteen weeks pregnant with our fifth child. My goal was to relax! All of a sudden, as he was drinking his coffee and looking out over the water, Tim popped up and shouted, "Dolphins. They can't be that far away. I gotta go see!" And without a second thought, he picked up his snorkel gear. He hopped the wall and headed down to the shore.

As I watched from our balcony, sipping my orange juice, I thought to myself, *That would be really cool to see dolphins in the wild. Wow! What a neat experience.* But despite Tim's enthusiasm, I knew how far out into the ocean I would need to go. I knew I wouldn't be able to see the bottom. Fear set in. That day, though, my excitement overcame my fear. I grabbed my snorkel gear and rushed out. Tim was already halfway there, but I could still see the dolphins jumping.

That swim was grueling. But the reward of swimming in the open ocean with thirty-plus dolphins, including babies, was worth the effort and worth going into the unknown. The sounds I heard, the beauty I experienced, and the exhaustion that followed made it a lifetime memory. I learned something that day: beyond my comfort zone is beauty I'll never see if I don't step out. We see one thing; God sees another. And I don't want to be so stuck in my comfort zone that I miss the things God has for me that might change my life forever.

Let's walk forward into this week aiming to be a little bit more like Nehemiah: tuned in to the Lord, listening for His calling, responding when He sets a dream in our hearts, and moving forward in faith for what God sees that we don't. He knows what lies ahead of us even when we have no idea.

Pray

Dear Lord, sometimes you call me into new territory that feels uncomfortable. I can be hesitant to do what You call me to, knowing it may stretch me and I may even face opposition. But, God, I want to be like Nehemiah. I want to be tuned in to You, to hear Your calling in my life, and to go where You want me, even if I can't quite see the other side. Help me to trust in You and trust in Your plans and purposes for me, Lord. In the name of Jesus, I pray against the lies of the enemy. Whatever You call me to, Lord, I know You will equip me for it. When You set a dream in my heart, help me recognize that it's from You! Thank You that beyond my comfort zone are new ways that You will stretch my heart and mind. You've already won the victory, Lord, and I want to be part of Your Kingdom movement here on earth to pack out heaven! In Jesus' name, amen.

Miracles point us to Jesus. They are meant to glorify God as the sole source of our hope and faith.

15

God Still Works Miracles

Jesus Christ is the same yesterday, today, and forever.

HEBREWS 13:8

HAVE YOU EVER TRIED listing all the miracles you've witnessed or experienced in your life? I'm talking real "only God could do that" miracles. It's a pretty cool thing to do. Here are a few that my family and I have experienced:

My nephew, born at twenty-nine weeks, is now thriving.

That same nephew needed open-heart surgery, and God ordained the exact surgeons to be at the hospital that day to perform the surgery.

My niece was born not breathing. Doctors said she would have brain damage, but she is now a healthy preteen.

Another nephew was found to have a complete heart block in the womb and was not expected to survive. Today he's doing well.

My father-in-law survived a massive stroke against all odds.

My brother got in a terrible car accident that left him brain-dead. Fourteen days later, he went home fully functioning.

My sister-in-law's heart stopped after she gave birth. No one knew why. Her organs shut down, and doctors said she would need multiple organ transplants. They later found a small, rare tumor and removed it. Four months later, she walked out of the hospital.

Not to mention the miracle of life every time I have birthed a child! We can probably each count so many miracles in our lives, and the reality is that miracles can't be measured. Whether it feels big or small, a miracle is a miracle. As much as I've experienced the miracles above, I've also experienced forgiveness when I don't deserve it, financial provision in difficult times, and of course the miracle of finding my car keys when I'm in a hurry to leave. If you look for them every day, you will find them every day. But in the same breath that I list out these miracles, I could tell you that sometimes it seems like God doesn't perform the same type of miracles today that He did when Jesus walked the earth. Or maybe we think He does still perform miracles, but they usually happen in other countries or remote villages—certainly not in our church or community.

What is a miracle, anyway? Does it have to be earth-shattering? Or does God work everyday miracles too? You and I may never know the answers to these questions. And maybe they're not even the right questions. What if we asked this question instead: "What does a miracle do?" The obvious answer may be that it miraculously heals someone from an injury or disease. On a deeper level, though, miracles point us to Jesus. They are meant to glorify God as the sole source of our hope and faith.

Faith is an activator for miracles as well. In the Bible, we read the story of the Roman centurion whose slave was sick (see Luke 7:1-10). The centurion sent a message to Jesus, asking Him to come heal his slave. While Jesus was on the way to the house, the centurion sent Jesus another message: "Lord, don't trouble yourself by coming to my home, for I am not worthy of such an honor. I am not even worthy to come and meet you. Just say the word from where you are, and my servant will be healed" (Luke 7:6-7). What faith, right? Even Jesus said He hadn't seen anyone with faith like that in all of Israel (see Luke 7:9), and Jesus was surrounded by a lot of faith-filled people.

Faith activates miracles, but miracles also build faith. They are meant to be shared to encourage believers and show people what Jesus is like. Can you imagine the joy of seeing someone completely healed? Maybe you can. I can because I've seen it. And when I share the stories of miracles my family and I have experienced, people are in awe. Whether they believe in God or not, they recognize that these miraculous healings are out of the ordinary. The more we share our testimony and stories of God's goodness and miraculous power in our lives, the more people are drawn to the Lord.

Miracles display God's glory and help His Kingdom to expand! Miracles also open our hearts to the Lord. When we acknowledge God's miracle-working power, we acknowledge what He is capable of. Miracles remind us that no matter how out of control we feel, God is still in control. This doesn't mean that God is the kind of God who does whatever we want when we snap our fingers. No, His purposes and plans may not look the way we anticipated. They may not even be what we want. But the closer we lean to Jesus, the more we have faith that God knows what He is doing.

Maybe you're in a tough spot today. You may doubt that God will answer you, do what He promised, or see you through to the other side. Be encouraged that Jesus "is the same yesterday, today, and forever" (Hebrews 13:8), which means His power hasn't changed and neither have His purposes or plans. He is the same miracle-working God that He is in the Bible. We just need to acknowledge what He has already done to remind ourselves of what He can (and will) still do.

Miracles are happening all around the world today. Babies are born, cancer is healed, people are protected from harm, and relationships that you thought were gone are restored. I know, for me, I tend to think of miracles in terms of people being healed from major diseases (which is true!), but God is so much bigger and broader than that. Which means our prayers to God can also be bigger and broader. He can handle them. Let's have faith that God can do what He has done before. Like the centurion, we can say, "I know what You are capable of, God, and I believe you can just say the word for a miracle."

Let's walk forward into this week praying that God will give us a miracle where we need it. I encourage you to write down a list of miracles that you or someone you know has experienced. Use that as a faith builder for what's next, and pray in a way that acknowledges who God is and what He still does when we align with His purposes and plans for our life.

Pray

Dear Lord, thank You that You are God over the big and the small details in my life and in the world. Even when life lets me down, You don't. You are the same God who performed all the miracles we read about in the Bible, and You are still working in miraculous ways today. Thank You that Your plans and purposes are exactly as they should be. Because I trust You for that, I trust You'll work miracles in my life. I pray that I would recognize Your power and see all the miracles around me. That my faith would be built up so I would remember who You are and what You do for me. Thank you for Your miraculous power. Give me wisdom and protect my mind from the lies of the enemy. You are faithful, God. In Jesus' name, amen.

God is likely to teach us something different with each new beginning.

16

Things Will Still Bloom

Forget all that—it is nothing compared to what I am going to do. For I am about to do something new. See, I have already begun! Do you not see it? I will make a pathway through the wilderness. I will create rivers in the dry wasteland.

ISAIAH 43:18–19

IT WAS MID-JULY, and I hadn't yet planted our little vegetable gardens that I normally start at the beginning of June. It seems so silly, but this bugged me—no matter how much Tim tried to let me off the hook. It was something that really didn't take much time, yet I still hadn't fit it in. I started to guilt myself about all the times I could've done it and had instead chosen to do something else. By this point, I just wanted to say "Whatever" and pick it up the next year. There is an art to letting things go and being okay with that.

But there is also something in my personality that can't just forget about something so easily. My tendency is to pack it all in and make the most of every day, to keep up with traditions and things I've done in years past. Over the last couple of years, though, I've been learning about seasons and shifts—that I can let certain things go and start when I start. Sometimes letting myself off the hook is healthy. Still . . . I wanted my garden to grow!

And as I stared at those garden beds, wishing they would plant themselves, my husband said, "Just start, Sarah. Why does it matter when? You aren't too late, and things will still bloom." *Things will still bloom.* Wow, that hit me. Here I was a month and a half late to planting seeds, and I figured it was too late for anything to happen—yet my husband saw it differently. My seeds would just bloom a little later than other people's. *Things will still bloom.*

There have been many moments in my life when I felt like I wasn't blooming while everyone else was. I'm betting you've felt that way too. Friends are getting married, yet you are still single. Babies are being born, yet you are struggling to conceive. People are finding community in churches, and you are still searching for where God wants you to land. Other marriages seem to be thriving, and for some reason you're just not in sync with your spouse right now. Does all of this mean you are too late to bloom? Absolutely not.

As a parent, I've also noticed my kids blooming at different paces. Every child does things at their own speed, yet as a culture we are consumed with milestones. Are they rolling by two months? Sitting up by six months? Crawling by eight months and walking by twelve months? Why is your child not saying 57 words by 19 months?

This isn't to condemn milestones; this is to condemn the idea that every single thing in life has to be a competition. It's easy to get caught up in a race to bloom without even realizing it. But the reality is we are all made uniquely in God's image, and no two people are alike. So, sure, milestones are great, but they shouldn't be the ultimate marker or goal in life. Living for the Lord should be our aim. Heaven should be our aim. Just because you haven't blossomed yet doesn't mean God hasn't planted things in you for His glory. He sure has (see Psalm 139:14), and maybe right now is a season of more planting. Maybe it's a season of growing deep roots. Maybe it's a season of hiding under the soil, completely protected until it's time to come up and blossom beautifully. If we rush the process and try to blossom too soon, we may wither away just as fast. Before blooming, don't you want to know that your roots are stable and strong?

You might feel like you are too little too late, but don't believe that lie. Whether in friendships, marriage, or parenting (or anything else for that matter), we are allowed to change our minds, shift gears, try something new, and even leave behind some old ways of doing things. It's okay to realize, *Hey, that worked well for me last time, but this time I'm going to try something different and see if it's a better fit.* We don't want to be flaky, but we do want to make sure that whatever season we are in, we are effectively living out God's purpose for us. Otherwise, we are dragging things in from the past and trying to make them work for the present. Square peg, round hole. They aren't always going to work. We have to start again and trust the Lord that the starting over will result in a fresh blossom in our lives. And God is likely to teach us something totally different with each new beginning.

The comfort of it all is that, as we desire and yearn for more, God is faithful. Our lives will be filled with many blooming seasons. They will also be filled with many seasons where blooms aren't visible, but growth is still happening. Both are needed, and both are healthy. So don't guilt yourself into quitting something before you even have a chance to start. Because, chances are, *things will still bloom*.

Let's walk forward into this week asking the Lord to show us the areas where He wants to work. Pray that He would prune back any areas of our lives that aren't serving His Kingdom. And then let's thank Jesus that He is faithful to tend to our hearts and grow us in a way that is far better than what we would've done ourselves.

Pray

Dear Lord, thank You so much that You know me better than anyone. You see my life laid out before any of it happens, and You know the areas that are blooming and those still waiting to blossom. If there are areas in my life that need to be pruned, I ask You to do that. Help me to see that even if I feel behind, it's never too late when I trust in You because that's where the growth begins. I don't want to give up when I don't see fruit right away. Help me to know that forward progress is progress! In Jesus' name, amen.

We can use our God-given gifts to help propel and accomplish our God-given dreams.

17

A Dream Come True

You can make many plans, but the LORD's purpose will prevail.

PROVERBS 19:21

A COUPLE YEARS AGO, November was a memorable month for our family. Not because of a birthday or anniversary, but because we had a midweek dinner together—in a place that had once been just a long-term dream. A year before, it was nothing more than a grassy field. Now I was staring at a beautiful two-story white barn trimmed out in black with basalt columns at the entrance. It was more than I had pictured in my head—and no, it wasn't a barn for animals. This was a space where we could welcome people and have respite (and fun!). There, in the middle of the mostly done construction, I cried tears of thankfulness and deep, deep joy. Most people would've noticed that the kitchen cabinets weren't complete and some of the rooms were missing doors. But none of that mattered. All I saw was a dream come true.

Years before this day, Tim and I had talked casually about wanting to construct a building where our whole extended family could gather. A place where we could hang out, host large family dinners, and let the kids run free and play in the winter when it was too cold to do anything else. A place where we could invite other families to join us. We didn't know all the details; we just knew it was a dream.

That's the thing about dreams, isn't it? Sometimes the Lord places the outline of a dream in our head. We may not be able to picture it clearly yet, but we can trust that if it is truly from the Lord, He will see it through. God doesn't give us dreams for our benefit alone, although that is a bonus. Rather, He gives us dreams that will have an eternal impact for His Kingdom, just as He gives us gifts with the same goal. The cool part is our gifts and dreams work in tandem. We can use our God-given gifts to help propel and accomplish our God-given dreams. God is always about His Kingdom. That's His goal. It should be our goal too.

I have to tell you a little backstory. Years ago, when we got married, Tim and I moved to his hometown, where I knew pretty much no one. I was married to my dream man, yet nothing else was playing out as I thought it should. The years following, I dug myself into a pit. A pit where I used my words to tear down my husband instead of building him up. I was so desperate for what I thought I wanted that I was determined to force it. Not so shockingly, this led to discontentment and bitterness. Then one day (after a lot of days), I was offered the gift of forgiveness. My pit had gotten so deep, yet the only way out was back up. Slowly but surely, after I asked for forgiveness from God and the one I hurt most, my husband, rebuilding began. Never would I have imagined praying for the place I lived—I didn't even like it at first. But slowly and surely, I did just that. I began to pray from Jeremiah 29:5-7: peace and prosperity for the city God had sent me to.

From that point on, I saw God at work in my heart even though my circumstances were so different from what I'd originally hoped for. My heart began growing content in what the Lord had given me. Then two of my sisters moved to our town—which was something I wouldn't have even thought to pray for.

As Tim and I began to pray together about ways the Lord would use us, the dream of a gathering place for our family and friends came to the surface. We kept saying, "No, that's still years off," but the opportunity to build kept presenting itself in an obvious way. So we planted our roots deeper and listened. Twelve months from that moment, we found ourselves having our very first dinner in the new space, surrounded by loads of family. To many people, this would have looked like just another dinner, but to us, it was a God-sized dream realized. We pray that we will use it in a way that impacts the Kingdom of God for eternity.

I'm certain of one thing: I will never be able to predict what God has planned for each of us because my mind is so limited. But God's isn't. He sees us, and He sees the grand picture of our lives. He will weave in things unexpectedly and plant dreams in our hearts, and as things come together, we will say, "Ahhhh . . . now I get why that happened." But none of this is possible unless we are tuned in to the Lord. He is a patient God. If we choose to do things our own way, He's often going to let that play out. But when we turn to the Lord and say, "Your way, not mine," He will do His best work in our lives, *for our good* and always *for His glory*! You can count on that.

If you have a dream that God placed on your heart, praise the Lord! Keep walking in His truth, being diligent in the areas you've been called to. Keep praying, keep going, and keep trusting. The fruit will come when His timing is right. And the dream will turn out better than we imagine.

If you aren't sure what dreams God has for you, ask Him! James 1:5 is an all-time favorite verse because it gives us a glimpse of God's generosity and how He *loves* to give freely. So much so that James says here, "If you need wisdom, ask our generous God, and he will give it to you." What a promise. It's easy for people to read that and think, *God will give me wisdom all the time no matter what.* If we keep going into verses 6 and 7, though, we read, "But when you ask him, be sure that your faith is in God alone. Do not waver, for a person with divided loyalty is as unsettled as a wave of the sea that is blown and tossed by the wind. Such people should not expect to receive anything from the Lord." *Do not waver*—not in relying on God, not in developing your giftings, not in pursuing God-given dreams. None of it! Live out the dreams He's placed in you, and trust Him to provide for you every step of the way.

Let's walk forward into this week laying our own dreams at the feet of Jesus. In exchange, let's ask God to give us new dreams that bring Him glory. While we're at it, let's also ask Him for help to achieve those dreams!

Pray

Dear Lord, thank You for the deep joy I experience through the dreams You've given me. Please help me to be open to the things You have for me instead of trying to formulate happiness through my own efforts. Would You take the dreams in my heart and align them with Yours? If they aren't what You have for me, please help me lay them down, knowing that what You promise and plan is far better than what I think up. Father, when You lay a dream on my heart, please equip me with the tools to make it happen. Connect me with other like-minded believers whose aim is packing out the Kingdom of Heaven. Thank You for Your deep love for me and that You plant God-sized dreams in the hearts of those who turn to You. I want to be one of those people. Help me, Lord! In Jesus' name, amen.

Whatever you are facing right now, take comfort in knowing that God faces it with you, walks alongside you, and even goes ahead of you.

18

What Is God Like?

> The Lord came down in a cloud and stood there with him; and he called out his own name, Yahweh. The Lord passed in front of Moses, calling out, "Yahweh! The Lord! The God of compassion and mercy! I am slow to anger and filled with unfailing love and faithfulness."
>
> EXODUS 34:5-6

IF YOU COULD DESCRIBE GOD IN ONE WORD, WHAT WOULD IT BE? Awesome? Kind? Angry? Understanding? Empathetic? Strict? Maybe faithful or possibly distant? How we view Him is likely a reflection of our experiences with Him, for better or for worse. Just like with any person we know, there are so many characteristics that make up God—which should get us excited. He's not a one-sided God who can't relate to us. Quite the opposite. He's multifaceted and shows Himself in so many ways. In our thriving seasons, it's much easier to identify God's powerful and mighty ways. When we are walking through a trial, it's easier to forget what type of God we serve.

Emotions are real, but they often cloud our thinking. I like to say feelings are finicky. They can send us this way and that, slapping us around from wave to wave of varying emotions. First joy, then sadness, followed by contentment, which is quickly overcome by fear of what may come. This is a prime example as to why we shouldn't put all our stock in our feelings. Because while feelings are a good gift from God, they can also be unreliable as a source of truth. Feel them, sure. But then line them up against the truth of who God says He is.

If we're going to do that, it's important that we actually know who God is. What are His characteristics? We can get to know God through His Word, the Bible. Scripture is God's truth, so we can count on the fact that it is reliable and always stays the same (no matter how anyone feels about it).

The Bible has lots of ways to describe God that we should absolutely know about. God is love. God is just. These characteristics apply to every situation God's people find themselves in. But the Bible also notes when God does *exactly* what His people need Him to do in that moment. The same is still true for us today. God never changes, but He is also exactly who you need Him to be in your own life. He understands everything about our lives and is always relevant because of His omniscience, omnipotence, and omnipresence. Let's take a look at a few examples from the Bible:

When Abraham was establishing his territory, God walked with Abraham as his friend.

When Moses led the Israelites out of Egypt, they complained about the lack of food. So God sent manna to nourish them. God was their provider.

When Joshua went out to battle time and time again to conquer a city God told him to defeat, God was his shield and defender.

When Job lost everything, God was his redeemer and restorer.

Want to see some more of who God is? Of course you do. Because the more we know about the God we serve, the more exciting living for God becomes. Each description below is mentioned in Scripture:

Wonderful Counselor, Prince of Peace, Mighty God, Holy One, gentle, loving, gracious, compassionate, slow to anger, abounding in love and faithfulness, infinite, great, unchanging, all powerful, full of wisdom, faithful, good, perfect, just, righteous, upright, merciful, radiant, powerful, personal, creator, jealous for His people, anchor of our soul, shield, comforter, judge, overcomer, refuge, conqueror.

Can you imagine knowing someone like this? If you met someone with all those qualities, wouldn't you want to be with them all the time, knowing they would never let you down? It's hard to imagine because no one on earth is that way. Our minds only know what they know. But of course you would want to be consistently near them. You might just think you hit the jackpot of relationships. And you would be right. Naturally, you would tell others all about this person—and they would probably want to meet this person too! That's the power of sharing about who our God is.

Knowing who God is also helps us as we walk through various seasons of struggle and triumph. When we grieve the loss of someone or something dear to us, God is our comforter. When we struggle financially, God is our sustainer. When we receive a clean bill of health after months or years of battling a disease, we recognize that God is our faithful healer. When everything around us is shaky and chaotic, God is our peace that passes all understanding.

None of this means God is a genie in the sky who does whatever we want. But as we get to know Him better through His Word, we learn that He is trustworthy and at work for our good. The benefits of knowing who God is are more than we can imagine and enough to cover us for a few lifetimes. Plus there is more than enough of God's kindness to share with others, and that's exactly what He wants us to do. Whatever you are facing right now, take comfort in knowing that God faces it with you, walks alongside you, and even goes ahead of you.

Let's walk forward into this week focusing on one characteristic of God that He has been to us lately. Thank Him for being who He says He is and for being faithful even when no one else is. Pray that you would know God more intimately and that, as you read the Bible, He would reveal His qualities to you!

Pray

Dear Lord, You are so good to me. I don't deserve any of what You give, yet because You are a generous God, You provide everything I need. Not only that, but You see me where I am, and nothing takes You by surprise. Thank You for being my rescuer, my peace, my joy, my hope, merciful, slow to anger, forgiving, just, and righteous. I know that no matter what I face, You will face it with me, never leaving me nor forsaking me. Father, help me not to forget who You are. I want to share You with everyone I know because I want to be part of Your plan. As I grow to know You more, help me to be an image bearer of the qualities You possess so Your love, goodness, and mercy can flow through me to others, making them want to know You more. Lord, I ask that You would bring peace and hope into my heart and build me up in You. In Jesus' name, amen.

Whatever the Lord has gifted you to do, do it!

19

Don't Be an End Cap

A generous person will prosper; whoever refreshes others will be refreshed.

PROVERBS 11:25, NIV

GOD CALLS ME TO ____________. Fill in your own blank. We all have been given different talents and giftings, so everyone's answer will be a little bit different. I love that about God. Our talents are unique to us. God doesn't make mistakes. He knew exactly what He was doing with you, with each of us.

One of the things Tim is really good at (and since I'm his wife, I can tell you he's good at a lot of things) is irrigation work. Now that may not sound like a big deal to many, but it sure has saved us lots of money as we've developed our property slowly but surely over the years. I've watched Tim map out his plans, dig trenches, lay pipes, and glue them together. Then he holds his breath and turns on the water, hoping everything goes as it should. Usually, he doesn't get it all on the first go-round, but with enough adjustments and tweaking, soon we have a fully functioning sprinkler system. I'm always blown away by all the work, but Tim always walks away and says, "Oh, it's no big deal." That's just Tim.

But I want to tell you something interesting I've learned from watching Tim lay hundreds of pieces of pipe on our property. Pipes come in many different shapes and sizes. Some are straight, some look like the letter T, and some are end caps. I distinctly remember a specific time I was praying, and I felt God give me this thought of *not* being an end cap with my giftings. *What does that mean, Lord?*

End caps, by nature, are just that: the end of something flowing. They simply catch whatever comes their way and sit there at the end collecting—never pouring out. I don't want to be someone God pours into but who does nothing with what He's given me. What's the point of the gifting if nothing comes out of it? It's a waste. But if I'm being fruitful, so much can come out of that. Especially when it's used to impact others for the Lord and pack out heaven. Instead of being an end cap, we can choose to be a piece of God's Kingdom that connects both ways so God can pour into us, knowing the blessing will continue to flow to others. I want to be that kind of part and use whatever I've been given to show God's goodness to others!

We threw a movie night one time and gave everyone free tickets to our concession stand. The kids were thrilled. As an extra, we challenged the kids to memorize Matthew 7:18-20. These verses talk about how a good tree can only bear good fruit and a bad tree can only bear bad fruit. I loved the conversations this brought up with my children about how we ought to live our lives. The more we pour into, nourish, feed, and grow the talents and abilities God has given us, the more He can work through us to accomplish His will, which changes our hearts in the process.

Think about what natural giftings and bents God has given you, and then consider how you can use those to share the love of Jesus. Are you great in the kitchen? Maybe take a meal or a fresh loaf of bread to someone once a month. Are you artistic? Maybe design a card and send it to someone who's struggling. Imagine how that will make their day. Are you an encourager? Some of my friends are so amazing at just sending a text to check in or to say, "I'm praying for you." The kindness of those friends impacts me greatly just when I need it most.

Whatever the Lord has gifted you to do, do it! Bear good fruit of love, joy, and kindness—and share it with others. When you do, they may start bearing good fruit too, and the impact for heaven will widen with each person along the way. It just keeps getting better. Conversely, the less we use our gifts, the less effective we become. Think of lifting weights and gaining muscle. Muscle won't just stick around if we don't put in training and time. Practice makes better, and the more we put in the time and effort to practice and use our natural giftings, the more naturally they come.

Let's walk forward into this week with the goal of filling in that blank: *God calls me to* ________. Once you identify at least one gifting that you can use to bless others, you'll be ready to go. Find a way this week to bless someone else, and remember—let's not be end caps. Let's be the straight or the T-shaped pipes that allow what God's given us to flow right through and into the lives of others. No sense keeping all of it to ourselves!

Pray

Dear Lord, thank You that when You formed me, You made no mistakes. You put giftings and talents inside me so I could live out Your purpose in my life. Help me to listen to You and to understand what You have called me to do. When that becomes clear, help me to use those giftings to walk in Your plan for me. I know it will be good because You are good. You have been faithful my whole life, so I want to be faithful to allow what You've given me to flow through to others. Lord, help me not to be an end cap. Help me to be a conduit of Your love and kindness to the world. In Jesus' name, amen.

The more I practice flexibility, the more it feels like a shortcut to genuine joy.

20

The Joy of Flexibility

My old self has been crucified with Christ. It is no longer I who live, but Christ lives in me. So I live in this earthly body by trusting in the Son of God, who loved me and gave himself for me.

GALATIANS 2:20

CAN I TELL YOU SOMETHING about myself? I may not look organized—or so I'm told based on the clutter on my desk, ha! But my personality loves to have everything in order. So, in my head, I'm organized. I don't make checklists and to-do lists every day, but I have rhythms and routines to my day that help our family stay the course. But even with all the rhythms and all the routines, consistency won't always breed contentment. Sometimes the best plans get sidelined . . . and the result is even better than you could've planned. You with me?

I often get an idea in my head and focus on making it happen exactly how I envision it. But motherhood and the Lord have a way of humbling you. For example, at Christmastime, I love matching jammies. In my head, I picture setting up and decorating the tree as a family in our Christmas jammies, with music blasting and everyone having the most joyful time. So when one kid can't find his pajamas, the baby is exhausted and still napping, or someone is not feeling their best, it can be hard to get out of my head and redirect the plans I had. But if there is one thing I've learned over and over through the years, it's that the ability to pivot can often bring greater joy than the stubbornness to stick with the plan. And sometimes it's in the pivoting that we discover even better outcomes than we planned for ourselves. In my case, extra snuggles on the couch while watching a Christmas movie have made for the best unplanned memories.

Would matching jammies and no sick kiddos have brought ultimate joy? No. Because true joy—God's joy—isn't found in perfectly planned evenings.

What I've realized is this: the more I'm willing to be flexible, the more joy I actually experience. Of course, I still enjoy things that go according to plan, but that becomes less and less important. The more I practice flexibility, the more it feels like a shortcut to genuine joy.

Do you find that you get caught up in routines and plans and checklists only to get to the end of a day or week and realize you never stopped to enjoy the moments? Maybe you just check-marked your way through them. And although you accomplished much, you really don't feel a sense of accomplishment. The completion may fulfill you temporarily, but not long-term. Because it's not sustainable.

My father-in-law used to visit our house four or five times a week. He never stayed more than twenty or thirty minutes, but those visits were my favorite. He is a man who loves the Lord deeply and is full of wisdom. We had conversations about all sorts of things. If I had a decision to make—whether big or small—one of his favorite things to say was "Well, you may just have to call an audible." That meant I might need to change my plans based on my circumstances. I can't tell you how many times I've thought, *Well, that's not going to work anymore* and shifted plans. Things like naptimes, potty training, and rough days with difficult attitudes will do that to you.

When my father-in-law had a stroke, everything changed. Our whole family had to call an audible on life. Big plans paused, events were canceled, ideas changed about what the future may look like. But you know what else happened? Those audibles—those pivots from what we knew—ended up bringing some of the biggest blessings to our family personally and broadly. We moved to live nearby (as in next-door nearby), and the kids got more time with Grandma and Grandpa, who were home a lot more now. We realized how quickly life can change, and we learned the value of taking pictures in the moment to preserve our memories. We ditched the idea that everything had to be "just so" to make it special and instead embraced all the mishaps along the way. Most of all, we relied on the Lord to be our peace in the middle of what felt like the biggest pivot of our lives.

God never changes His purposes or plans in our lives. He's always been a plan A God! But He often exchanges the things we think we need for the things He's promised to give us. Isaiah 61:3 says God gives us beauty for ashes, "the oil of joy instead of mourning," "praise instead of a spirit of despair" (NIV). He exchanges our chaos for peace and gives us hope and joy. With God, you can always guarantee an "upchange," meaning what God gives is better than what we originally thought we needed.

Let's walk forward into this week seeing if there are any areas where we need to pivot. Is there something in our lives that isn't producing good fruit? Maybe it's time to cut it off and ask the Lord to give us a new direction. And when He does, let's put our whole heart and whole trust in where He takes us!

Pray

Dear Lord, I can be so darn stubborn, and I'm so sorry for that. Will You forgive me? Thank You for continuing to teach me that the ability to pivot is such a gift. That when my plans go awry, You can give me the flexibility I need. I'm so grateful that I can exchange what *I* think is best for what *is* best for my family and Your Kingdom. Lord, help me understand that perfectly laid plans don't guarantee joy, but You do. I want to rest in Your peace and maintain an attitude of peace over perfection in my life. Please help me remember what's most important: growing Your Kingdom and living as You've called me to. I want to stay humble in my walk with You, Lord, and guide my family to do the same. In Jesus' name, amen.

Four key things needed to fall into place: knowledge, wisdom, understanding, and favor.

21

K.W.U.F.

The LORD grants wisdom! From his mouth come knowledge and understanding.

PROVERBS 2:6

MY FATHER-IN-LAW was an entrepreneur for the longest time, and he definitely passed that gifting on to my husband. He always had six or seven ideas in his head at any given time, and it was fun to hear how he dreamed big for the Lord, his family, and his business.

One time, he walked into our house and out of nowhere said, "Kuhwoof." I wanted to say "Bless you" but instead said "What?" And he repeated himself again. Soon he clarified he wasn't making sneezing sounds or barking like a dog. Instead, he had come up with an acronym. He wasn't actually saying "Kuhwoof" but "K.W.U.F." He proceeded to tell me that, as he was praying the other day, the Lord told him that for every decision he made, four key things needed to fall into place: knowledge, wisdom, understanding, and favor. Then he would pray about whether he should say yes at that time. Let's take a look at each letter.

K: Knowledge. Read Psalm 119:66 and Proverbs 15:14. The first speaks of asking the Lord to teach us knowledge. The second speaks of being hungry for knowledge. Are we willing to learn when the Lord (or someone else) teaches us something? Do we listen or ignore Him? Then, are we willing to look for all the information and knowledge surrounding our decisions? Do we look multiple places and not just to one biased source? Do we have all the facts? Let's do our due diligence and prayerfully gather all the information we need to equip us in good decision-making.

W: Wisdom. The Bible says that wisdom is better than gold (see Proverbs 16:16). That's a pretty lofty claim. The Bible also makes it clear that wisdom is from the Lord and not from people (see 1 Corinthians 3:19). It also says, "The foolishness of God is wiser than human wisdom" (1 Corinthians 1:25, NIV). Isn't it amazing that the wisdom of all the wisest people on earth doesn't even come close to the wisdom of our God? James 1:5 says, "If you need wisdom, ask our generous God, and he will give it to you. He will not rebuke you for asking." How cool is that? We can and should go to God with any questions, knowing that He will give us wisdom for every possible situation.

U: Understanding. In the Bible, understanding always seems to follow wisdom or knowledge. So it makes sense that we need both of those before we can gain understanding. Once we have the knowledge and wisdom to make a decision, understanding allows us to know how our decision will affect us and those around us. As with the first two, understanding comes from the Lord. Proverbs 3:5 tells us not to lean on our own understanding. Understanding from the Lord helps us to obey His commands, which ultimately helps us to stay in His will and on His path for our lives.

F: Favor. Last but not least is favor, which might be the trickiest of them all. The word *favor* gets misused and tossed around like confetti—so much so that no one wants to believe it is actually real. Real favor is God's grace, and it cannot be earned—only received. When it comes to making decisions, a good prayer to pray is, "Lord, if this is Your will, show favor to all those involved in this decision, and give us favor every step of the way—for Your glory and not our gain." Favor should be for His glory, not our gain. Period.

I can easily walk into daily decisions without a second thought. I have to make many decisions as I'm trying to hustle through the day and get things done. Decisions like what to make for lunch or when to run errands don't always need major prayer or the K.W.U.F. assessment. But many decisions require us to dig deeper and ask the Lord for help. That's why I love the practical (and biblical) idea of running through these four letters. They may not give us the final yes or no, but they can help. K.W.U.F. shows me how to pursue the Lord's will rather than my own, and that's exactly where I want to stay.

Let's walk forward into this week changing how we make decisions. Try applying K.W.U.F. to whatever you are facing, and ask the Lord to help you and pause before moving forward.

Pray

Dear Lord, thank You so much that every single good thing comes from You—and that includes good decision-making. I make decisions every day, and because of that, I want You involved. I want You to teach me how to walk in Your knowledge, Your wisdom, and Your favor so I can see Your purpose and will for my life. Before I make big decisions, help me to pause and ask You for each of these things. Once I hear from You, help me to know if what I'm facing is a best yes for the season I'm in. I pray You would protect my mind and heart from confusion and help me keep my feelings in check, knowing that Your truth is what I want to rely on in my life. In everything I do, I want to have an eternal impact. In Jesus' name, amen.

They feel *joy* for the fact that they were forgiven.

22

Reason to Rejoice

Oh, what joy for those whose disobedience is forgiven, whose sin is put out of sight! Yes, what joy for those whose record the LORD has cleared of guilt, whose lives are lived in complete honesty!

PSALM 32:1–2

I BET MOST PEOPLE wouldn't put the words *joy*, *disobedience*, and *forgiven* in the same sentence. But David did. In fact, he almost makes forgiveness sound exciting. That's because it is—or it should be, at least. I usually feel sad or ashamed when I think of forgiveness—that when we're forgiven, we should sulk around for a bit and really let it sink in. Based on what David says in this psalm, though, I don't think that should be our normal response.

When my kids ask forgiveness—either from me or from one another—I notice a common theme. They ask forgiveness for whatever the offense was, and then they hug and bounce off happily, back to whatever they were doing. They don't tend to carry the guilt with them or let it weigh them down. They feel *joy* for the fact that they were forgiven. Don't you just love that? Don't you wish we could all respond the same way? Well, the good news is we can absolutely take joy in being forgiven and knowing that we are cleared of guilt. That doesn't mean we keep doing the same disobedient thing over and over—no! Read the last five words of John 8:11: "Go and sin no more." We are called to ask for forgiveness, then turn from that sin and live in complete honesty.

I'd also like to point out that asking for forgiveness is more than just saying "I'm sorry." We have a saying in our house: "I'm sorry" is for accidents; "Forgive me" is for when it's intentional. If one of my kids is walking down the hallway and accidentally bumps into one of their siblings who then starts crying, it was an accident. So I expect that the person who did the bumping will check on their sibling and make sure that they are okay followed by an "I'm sorry. That was an accident."

But if one of our kids is walking down that same hallway and they stick out their elbow to jab their sibling, thinking it's funny, that's obviously intentional and requires a different response. "Will you please forgive me for sticking out my elbow and making you fall?" I want you to note two things here: I expect the child to apologize for what happened and to say out loud what they did. This acknowledges their exact actions, which makes clear to them how yucky the sin was. We tend to repeat sin when we don't have to own up to it or tell anyone about it. Speaking the sin out loud can propel us to turn the other way and make a better choice the next time. I also tell my kids to ask God for forgiveness, because He is the one ultimately making us clean.

Once we confess the sin out loud to people and to the Lord, we are doing what David said and living in complete honesty. This is reason to rejoice! We can say hallelujah to the fact that we don't have to walk around guilty, carrying the weight of our sin. Once we acknowledge the offense and ask for forgiveness, we can live out Psalm 32. Our disobedience is forgiven (oh, what joy!), our sin is put out of sight (oh, what joy!), our record is cleared of guilt (oh, what joy!), and we get to live our lives in complete honesty (oh, what joy!).

This week, don't delay asking forgiveness if you need to. Go ask for it, receive it, and walk away free from that guilt. If you aren't sure whether you need to seek forgiveness, ask the Lord to help you see any people you have hurt. If He does reveal something to you, don't feel shame. Feel joy that you have the opportunity to clear your record of any guilt.

Pray

Dear Lord, You are a God who gives good gifts, and one of those is the gift of forgiveness. Thank You for offering it freely when I come to You with a repentant heart. Lord, please reveal anything I need to seek forgiveness for, whether from someone else or from You. Show me the areas where sin has crept in. I don't want to walk around carrying the weight of that sin when You died to free me from it. I want to live in the joy of obedience and forgiveness that You promise. I want to live in complete honesty, knowing that even when I make mistakes, You forgive me. Because of Your work in my life, I can aim not to stumble again in the same way. God, I want to live in a way that's different from the world. I want to live Your way! Help my heart to be willing to respond and change to be more like You. Thank You for living a sinless life, dying on the cross for my sins, forgiving me, and allowing me to live in Your freedom. I'm eternally grateful. In Jesus' name, amen.

We can
posture
ourselves
toward
the Lord,
and we can
encourage
our kids to
do the same.

23

God Looks at the Heart

The LORD said to Samuel, "Don't judge by his appearance or height, for I have rejected him. The LORD doesn't see things the way you see them. People judge by outward appearance, but the LORD looks at the heart."

1 SAMUEL 16:7

TWO LONG YEARS. At least they felt long from a parenting perspective. For the first two years of his life, one of our kids struggled more than all the rest combined. I'm not talking discipline struggles; I'm talking health struggles. Poor guy got sick as an infant, and for the next two years we battled sickness after sickness for what seemed like 75 percent of each month with minimal relief. We snuggled, held, rocked, soothed, stayed up late, carried him everywhere, and rarely put him down because his little body just couldn't handle breathing well without medicines. Unfortunately, the medicines only gave short-term relief. Because his breathing was labored, his endurance was low. Because his endurance was low, his energy was low. During the flare-ups, he seemed to spend all his energy breathing and just couldn't do much else. Talk about heartbreaking to watch your child go through that. On top of that, because he used his energy for living, he fell behind developmentally—and a lot of it showed up in the area of speech. Which carried with it a touch of mom guilt that there wasn't more I could do for him.

Church was one of the places we always held him. Our son didn't want to be put in kids' church without us no matter how much we tried. He was just very attached, and because of that, we held him through every service. When he got too distracting, we would take turns holding him out in the hallways. Can I be honest with you? This became really wearing on us. We love him so much, but it also meant that Tim and I didn't sit through a church service together for over a year and a half.

One day, my entire perspective changed. I was reading the Bible story of Samuel choosing a new king (see 1 Samuel 16:1-13). As Samuel looked over a family full of handsome and warrior-like brothers, he thought one of them must be the future king. Yet when he got to the end, God surprised him—He hadn't picked any of those young men. Samuel was shocked, but the Lord basically told him, "You are looking at physical attributes, but *I look at the heart.*" We later find out there was one more son—David. That day, the Lord chose David not based on his looks or stature but his heart.

One Sunday, during worship at our church, I looked over at our son and the most beautiful thing was happening. His eyes were shut, his little hands were raised in worship, and he was swaying back and forth. He was so clearly being touched by the Lord. In that moment, God spoke to me so clearly about our son. He told me that this whole time I had been worried about all the wrong things. The outside things. I was carrying around worry not just about his health but about when he would walk and talk and hit all the so-called milestones. And what mattered most to the Lord? None of that. It was like God spoke to me, *Sarah, it is so easy to look at your son and only see the outside. But I see his spirit. And I see what's being built inside of him—his love for Me and things you can't see—and* that *is what matters most to Me.*

Sure, God cares about other things too, but even more, He cares about what's on the inside. While I could only see the hard, our little one was developing other things. Unseen things. Heart things. God things. And in that moment, I caught a glimpse of the heart of God. I saw His child turned toward Him in a posture of worship, resting in Him. That's what our boy was doing. I knew it in my spirit. And God was so pleased.

When we look at our children or the young people in our lives, what do we see? Do we see their sports stats, piano recitals, ribbons, and trophies? Do we see their schedules and to-do lists each week? Or do we see their character developing? God isn't looking for professionals. He's not looking for people who have perfect clothes and say all the right things. He's looking for those who aim their hearts toward Him, tune in to Him through all circumstances, and trust that the strength of character developing inside us will take us much further than any external success will.

We can posture ourselves toward the Lord, and we can encourage our kids to do the same. We can close our eyes, lift our hands, soften our hearts, and place ourselves at the feet of Jesus. We can know that God is working in our hearts even when nothing is working around us. He's working in us even when no one else can see what's happening. There is so much we can see and judge from the outside. Yet just like Samuel, none of us really know what is going on in the hearts of others—only God knows that. And He sees the big picture that we need to fully trust in.

Let's walk forward into this week ridding ourselves of the idea that the external is all that matters and knowing that whatever God is doing on the inside is most important. And let's bear good fruit from the overflow of our heart.

Pray

Dear Lord, I'm so glad that You care about my heart first—not just my external circumstances. Help me to see that not only in my own life but in the lives of those around me. And help me to extend the same grace You extend to me when I'm going through changes in my life. Thank You, Lord, that the milestones of this world are insignificant compared to the goal of heaven. Help me aim my heart and my head toward heaven so I don't get caught up in the worries of this world. I know that's not easy, Lord, but You can help me do it. And, Father, I pray against any shame or guilt that has crept into my mind. Replace that with Your truth. In Jesus' name, amen.

When our ground is shaky and we need something solid to stand on, God's Word is that for us.

24

Fighting Fear

God has not given us a spirit of fear . . .
but of power, love, and self-discipline.

2 TIMOTHY 1:7

JUST ASK SOMEONE what they are afraid of, and most people could list two or three things right off the bat. I know I could. Lots of us are afraid of spiders, snakes, heights, or enclosed spaces. But there are many other fears that go beyond the surface. Things like fear of loneliness, fear of death, fear of public speaking, or fear of people you disagree with (I'm joking about that one, but maybe it is a real fear!). Some fears can be debilitating, and we often allow the fear of something to keep us from experiencing it or even experiencing God's goodness. I'm guilty of that!

In some instances, fear can be healthy in the right amounts. We always tell our kids to have a healthy fear of the ocean, knowing that it is much more powerful than even the best swimmer. The Bible talks about the fear of the Lord. That's often misconstrued as being scared of God, but fearing the Lord really means to be in awe of Him and have a respect for His power.

A few times in my life, though, I've really struggled with unhealthy fear. I would think up scenarios to go with my fears and lie down to sleep at night only to find myself struggling with nightmares. The thing is, I knew there was actually nothing to be afraid of. Yet the fear lingered. Thankfully, I knew that when fears flooded in, I could encourage myself and build myself up in truth.

One truth that really helped me was reminding myself that irrational fears are lies straight from the enemy. Fears change; they come and go. But we serve a

God who doesn't change, and His promises are the same as they've always been. When our ground is shaky and we need something solid to stand on, God's Word is that for us. It shows us the truth and trumps all the lies the devil might try to convince us of. Here are some verses that build me up when fear tries to take over:

> "Do not be afraid of the nations there, for the Lord your God will fight for you" (Deuteronomy 3:22).
>
> "Be strong and courageous! Do not be afraid and do not panic before them. For the Lord your God will personally go ahead of you. He will neither fail you nor abandon you" (Deuteronomy 31:6).
>
> "The Lord is my light and my salvation—so why should I be afraid? The Lord is my fortress, protecting me from danger, so why should I tremble?" (Psalm 27:1).
>
> "When I am afraid, I will put my trust in you. I praise God for what he has promised. I trust in God, so why should I be afraid? What can mere mortals do to me?" (Psalm 56:3-4).

A few more verses that you can use to fight fear are Psalm 34:4-8, Psalm 46:1-3, Psalm 115:11, and John 14:27.

I find that reading these verses to myself is great, but speaking them out loud is even better. Sometimes it can feel funny to speak verses out loud, but words have power. Although it may start as a forced habit, repeating Scripture to counteract fear soon becomes natural, and we begin to fight like Ephesians 6:12 says we should. (Go look that one up!)

We can also take practical steps to combat fear, such as cutting out things that feed the fear. When I was in my twenties and struggling with nightmares, I asked the Lord to take them away. I felt like He told me to stop watching certain crime shows. At first I thought that must be a mistake. The crime shows weren't real—I knew that. So how could they possibly be affecting me? But, sure enough, turning them off proved to be helpful. It's no surprise that whatever we consume can plant seeds inside of us, so we have to be so careful with what we take in. Whether it's social media, TV, books, or music, it all has an effect on us. So along with counteracting fear with God's truth, we can also counteract fear with practical habits. We need both because both carry wisdom, and together they help us defeat the lies of fear.

Let's walk forward into this week refusing to allow fear to take over our lives. Let's identify the fear, fight it with God's truth, and know that we can battle the lies of the enemy in both practical and spiritual ways.

Pray

Dear Lord, I don't want to be controlled by fear. I want to live in Your truth, knowing that You've already won the battle—which means I've won too as long as I keep You first. Lord, the next time a fear creeps in, I'll lay it at Your feet. I pray that You would exchange my fears for Your truth and that I would believe it and receive it. Lord, I also ask You to reveal to me any areas in my life that may be contributing to my fears—areas that I can practically cut out and not consume any longer. I know I often control what comes into my mind, and I want those to be things of You. Help me, Lord! In Jesus' name, amen.

The more we pray over our family, the more the Lord will begin working in their lives in ways seen and unseen.

25

Touchpoints

Pray in the Spirit at all times and on every occasion. Stay alert and be persistent in your prayers for all believers everywhere.

EPHESIANS 6:18

MY GUESS IS THAT MOST OF YOU reading this do laundry every week. Nod your head with me if it's true. I know I have plenty of laundry to keep me busy week after week. Between seven kids with activities, towels, and more . . . it sometimes feels like a full-time job just washing and drying—and don't even mention folding and putting away. That's an extra two to three business days if you ask me. Whew. I spend so much time doing laundry that one day I had an idea of how I could pass the time with purpose. And what I discovered was better than just listening to podcasts or music (although I do both of those too). I needed something different. Something more.

The other side of the story was that I also had been feeling compelled by the Holy Spirit to do a better job of praying for my family. I always start out with great intentions and ideas of how I'm going to accomplish this, only to let them fade away and forget about praying purposefully. But we are called to pray for others. It's a biblical command, so it's something we *should* be practicing daily. We are also called to pray without ceasing—in other words, "never stop praying" (1 Thessalonians 5:17). I'm sure you have so much going on in your life that remembering to pray sometimes becomes the last thing on your list. I can relate. But I also know it should be the first thing on our list. The Lord knows that we have enough to pray about daily to keep us in constant conversation with Him. And that's a good thing. Yet we don't always do it because we get distracted with all the other things happening.

So how can we follow God's commands and be obedient in the midst of our days? How can we get everything done in a day when we need to focus on talking to the Lord? No matter how you look at it, that feels like a lot! The cool part is that the same God who created the universe also created a way for us to live life in constant relationship with Him without compromising on anything we need to get done. It definitely takes sacrifice and discipline. Sometimes we have to say no to certain things we want to do in order to say yes to the Lord.

However, when we do obey God, He always does more for us than we could've thought up for ourselves. God wants us to do well in the everyday areas of our lives because He cares about us. But our goals aren't the most important thing. His goals are. And we have the opportunity to be part of them. I know I've often had it backward: I wonder how I can squeeze God into the pockets of leftover time each day when, instead, He should be the first thing.

I've gone through seasons (and still do) when I don't put the Lord first in my day, thinking I will squeeze in time with him during naps or before bed, and I can always tell by how my day goes. A little less peace, lots of hiccups seemingly out of nowhere, and then, much to my chagrin, I remember, *Ahhh . . . that's right, I haven't spent time with the Lord today.* Right after that thought, I sometimes feel guilty or frustrated with myself. I'm tempted to wait until the next day to start over, but I remember that God just wants us to start right where we are. So I ask the Lord for forgiveness, invite Him into whatever is left of the day, and aim to put Him first the following day. And the next and the next.

That day, as I was folding laundry, I asked the Lord to help me put Him first in my days and pray more consistently for my family. Within seconds, I felt a Holy Spirit–inspired idea drop into my head: use the laundry time to pray for my family. I could use the moments it took to fold each person's laundry to pray over that specific family member. How easy is that to remember? Whosever clothes you are touching, that's the person you pray for. I decided to call these my "touchpoints," and it immediately began making a difference for me. I mean, I'm doing laundry every day, so why not make use of that time?

This can be taken beyond laundry too. Put it into practice while you are making lunch for members of your family or while you are picking up toys or cleaning their room. Pick a different day of the week to pray for each person in your family. The possibilities are endless. This easy way to incorporate prayer will make a difference in your life and theirs. The more we pray over our family, the more the Lord will begin working in their lives in ways seen and unseen.

This is just a starting point. The Holy Spirit can (and will) give you your own inspired ideas on how you can uniquely pray for your family and invite the Lord into your everyday moments. If you want to use the idea of touchpoints, do it! If you come up with something else, great! Let's make sure our days don't go by without bringing our family before the Lord. If they do, we can be diligent to just start wherever we are and know that any forward progress is progress.

Let's walk forward into this week finding our own touchpoints to invite the Lord into our daily tasks. Commit to trying it for one week (or more!), and see the impact it has on your life and the lives of the people you pray for.

Pray

Dear Lord, I don't want to get so caught up in my day that I don't invite You in to my everyday life. You gave me life, and I want to honor You by putting You first and not giving You the last of me. When I put You first, my days go better and my relationship with You deepens. Father, I also want to be obedient to pray for my family. Thank You for the family You've given me. Thank You that I have the opportunity to cover them all in prayer every day—please give me ideas on how I can do that consistently. There is power in prayer, and I want to see it impact my family. Thank You for hearing me and helping me in this area. In Jesus' name, amen.

We know in part, but He knows fully what we need even when we don't see it.

26

The Bigger Picture

We know that God causes everything to work together for the good of those who love God and are called according to his purpose for them.

ROMANS 8:28

OUR SON KICKED AND PUSHED US AWAY as we tried to put the nebulizer mask on to give him medicine that would help him breathe. He didn't see it as helpful. He just saw us smothering his face with something uncomfortable that he would have to sit still for five minutes to inhale. Not so easy for a squirmy toddler. And I can tell you it was rarely easy or fun—especially since it happened multiple times most days.

I don't blame him, you know? He was only one and a half years old, and although his breathing was labored, he didn't understand what the medicine would do. No amount of convincing would do that. So we had to resort to distracting him. We would read books, sing songs, and make up funny dances. If all those failed, we would video-call grandparents to talk to him, show him pictures in our camera roll, and anything else we could think of. Basically, we got through it the best we could.

As he got older, though, some things shifted. It was like he suddenly understood that whatever was happening during those treatments actually made him breathe easier. He started relaxing, letting us put the nebulizer strap over his head and the mask over his little button nose and mouth. His grip wasn't tight anymore, his eyes were calm, and he didn't fight us. He just waited patiently and breathed deeply. Soon, distractions weren't as crucial, as he would patiently sit through the five to eight minutes of breathing treatments. Without words, he began to realize that what we were doing was helpful and not harmful. He *felt* the difference.

This story may be about breathing treatments, but it also illustrates how we as believers tend to act when it comes to God's will in our lives. We think we know what is best—that is, until we hit a wall, have a breakdown, things fall apart, and everything becomes labored instead of laid-back. God wants us to rest and trust in Him so we can recover and move forward in what He has for us. But we don't always see it that way because we don't have God's perspective. Instead of following God's lead, we kick, scream, push back, and get distracted easily. Nothing can convince us that there is something better out there when we think we have "what's best" figured out. We continue to go about our lives, laboring and toiling endlessly, only to realize we are making little progress. Instead of digging ourselves a tunnel, we end up digging a pit.

God has a better way. Once we realize He brings peace that passes understanding and guards our hearts, it's much easier to stay on God's path than to fight it. When we allow ourselves to breathe deeply of God's goodness and what He offers, the reward is a God who is faithful to stick with us through everything. Not only that, but He helps us to make forward progress in Him. I'm not saying it will all be easy, but I am saying God will be faithful to never leave us. Want to know another cool benefit? This one comes straight from Isaiah 54:17: "No weapon turned against you will succeed. You will silence every voice raised up to accuse you." Isn't that so great? When we stay in God's purposes, we stop fighting Him and we begin fighting against the enemy. And God doesn't just fight with us as our helper. He fights *for us*! Even better.

When I watched our son battle against the nebulizer, not even knowing what he was battling, it created a picture for me of how we are without the Lord. It's like we have a sword, but we are just swinging it every which way, hoping to hit whatever comes at us. But with God, we put on His armor. Our moves become more purposeful, and we have the power of Jesus' name to back us up. Let's be that kind of people.

The ones who know our purpose.

The ones who understand whom we are fighting.

The ones who are confident in the God we serve.

The ones who rest in Jesus, knowing that what He offers brings peace instead of discord.

Once our son realized where he could get relief, he started pointing to his nebulizer when he needed it. Before we knew it, he graduated to an inhaler. He would bring me the inhaler, and as I set it to his mouth, his eyes showed that he trusted me. That this was good. That this was helpful. Our relationship with God is the same. We know in part, but He knows fully what we need even when we don't see it. We just have to be willing to trust Him.

Let's walk forward into this week asking the Lord to forgive us for fighting Him instead of leaning in to what He has for us. Once we do that, let's determine to step into where the Lord is leading us, even when we don't see the bigger picture. Because we know God's plans are good and will bring glory to His name!

Pray

Dear Lord, I'm thankful that You see a bigger picture than I do—and that You are patient and willing to help me get where I need to be in You. I want to fully trust You with my whole life. I want to fully embrace the purposes and plans You have for me. I want to fully rest, knowing that You will come alongside me and fight my battles for and with me. Lord, would You help me mature in my relationship with You so I don't stay the same, never fully knowing what You have for me? Forgive me for resisting in areas where I couldn't see beyond my circumstances. I'm ready to be bold and live for You freely. In Jesus' name, amen.

Listening is
a skill, and
like any skill,
it's one that
we have to
practice.

27

Solid Rock

Anyone who listens to my teaching and follows it is wise,
like a person who builds a house on solid rock.

MATTHEW 7:24

GOD WON'T FAIL YOU. He just won't. Period. Exclamation point! It's not even an option with Him because that's not how He operates. We were singing in church the other day, and I thought about the words of the song where one line says, "I build my life on Jesus," and it's followed by "Christ is my firm foundation, the Rock on which I stand."[2] Now, sometimes in the Bible, God's people failed and tried to blame Him. But the reason they failed was disobedience: God set out rules and boundaries, and when His people didn't follow His commands, things didn't go well for them. I suppose sometimes we are the same way. But again, God will never fail us.

As the worship song says, when we put our trust in God, we can build our life on His firm foundation. This is so important. Jesus shares a story about it in Matthew 7:24-29. He explains that there are two types of people: those who build their house on the rock and those who build their house on the sand. Our family has a little experience with this, as the town we live in is mostly built on rock. Literally. When you dig more than six inches down, you hit giant boulders. It makes building a bit trickier because where do you put all the rocks? But it also makes building a little bit sturdier because you know that nothing is going to suddenly cave in. My husband has built three different buildings for us over the years, so it became normal to hear the *chink, clink* noise from his backhoe as

[2] Cody Carnes, "Firm Foundation (He Won't)," on *Firm Foundation (Live)*, performed by Cody Carnes, Sparrow Records, 2023.

he dug out different areas. If you ever drive onto our property and see a lot of rock walls, rock borders, and rock features, now you know why!

I felt a sense of comfort knowing that we didn't have to do any out-of-the-ordinary processes to make building happen. We knew our foundation would be solid no matter what. We get that same sort of comfort with Jesus. When your life is built on Christ, nothing is going to tear it down. Now, will you get pushed, swayed, and tossed around a bit? Probably. But He will keep you grounded in Him. Jesus says this about the house built on rock: "Though the rain comes in torrents and the floodwaters rise and the winds beat against that house, it won't collapse because it is built on bedrock" (Matthew 7:25).

How do we practically build our life on Christ? Jesus says, "Anyone who listens to my teaching and follows it is wise, like a person who builds a house on solid rock" (7:24). Two things I notice here. First, we have to listen. One major part of building our life on Christ is listening to what He tells us. That's tough for a chatterbox like me to admit. But it's true. We can listen through prayer, through worship, through reading the Word of God, even through community. Just like in any relationship, the more we listen, the more we learn to recognize God's voice. The more we learn to recognize God's voice, the quicker we are able to identify what He is speaking to us. The quicker we are able to identify what God is speaking to us, the sooner we are able to obey and follow His commands.

Listening is a skill, and like any skill, it's one that we have to practice. Find time in your day to simply listen to God. Turn off or put away distractions and choose to make a space and place where you listen to what God is saying. These quiet spaces aren't the only time God is going to speak to you, though. He will often speak to us in the middle of lots of noise. I've sure noticed that as a mom whose quiet times are more limited. But in order for us to make listening a habit, the quiet times are often necessary to learn to hear God's voice. Start small, go from there, then keep going!

The second part may be even tougher than the first. After we listen, we have to follow. That means we have to take action! The reason we do this is to obey

God's commands, which bring us wisdom. Putting God's call into action might be as simple as praying for someone. It might involve writing an encouraging note or making a meal to ease someone's load. I find that the first time always seems to be the most difficult when it comes to obedience. But before you know it, it becomes second nature. Maybe this sounds a bit scary to you right now, but when God calls you to something, He's not going to let you down. You'll see!

Once our hearts are tuned to God's voice and quick to obey, He begins to call us to even bigger things for His Kingdom. And because we know that every time God has called us to something, He has been faithful to see us through, we can rest knowing that He won't fail us in anything.

Let's walk forward into this week choosing a time to make space to listen for God's voice. Turn on some worship music while you chop veggies for dinner, while you shower and get ready for the day, or while you take a walk outside. And let the Lord know that you are listening. Do it with intention and excitement for how He is going to speak to you!

Pray

Dear Lord, thank You for being my firm foundation. I believe that You are who you say You are, and I know that as long as I choose to walk in obedience to Your voice, You will give me wisdom on how to live for Your Kingdom. I want to be able to discern what You are calling me to do so I can choose to obey and move forward into whatever You have for me. I know even when I've made a mistake or gotten off course, I can turn back to You. I'm excited for the things You have for me, Lord—even the ones I don't know about, because I trust You with all my heart. In Jesus' name, amen.

Work with all your heart. Because through that, God is honored.

28

Made to Work

Don't store up treasures here on earth, where moths eat them and rust destroys them, and where thieves break in and steal. Store your treasures in heaven, where moths and rust cannot destroy, and thieves do not break in and steal. Wherever your treasure is, there the desires of your heart will also be.

MATTHEW 6:19–21

LONG AGO, I WAS LISTENING to a sermon called "The Blessing of Hard Work." Now, it would be easy to turn that off and think it's not for us. I mean, God loves pouring out His blessings on us, right? So why should we have to work hard to get them? Because the reality is work is one of the things God created us to do. At the very beginning of time, when God created Adam and placed him in the Garden of Eden, God gave him jobs to do. Genesis 2:15 tells us, "The LORD God placed the man in the Garden of Eden to tend and watch over it." Adam's job may not look like the job you have (unless your job happens to be naming animals and tending the most beautiful garden on earth), but it was clearly a job nonetheless. Work wasn't a result of the Fall or an idea man came up with; it was God's idea.

Through Adam's work, God poured out His blessing. First, He allowed Adam to freely eat of any tree except the tree of the knowledge of good and evil (see Genesis 2:16-17). Second, He gave Adam a helper, Eve, as his wife (read about it all in Genesis 2:21-25). I'd say those are pretty good benefits for a first job, wouldn't you? God gives each of us specific blessings out of the work we do when we honor Him with it.

You might say, "Well, I have acquaintances or coworkers who don't honor the Lord at all in their work, and they seem to be blessed for it over and over.

They live easy, seemingly fulfilling lives." I hear you. But how do we define *easy* and *fulfilling*? The world's definition is a stark contrast to God's definition. The question then becomes this: Are earthly riches and gains worth more than the gift of eternity with God? Don't be fooled—they absolutely aren't. It may seem like others are storing up some pretty sweet blessings here on earth, but I guarantee you it will all be for nothing when we get to heaven and see what the Lord has stored up for us (see 1 Corinthians 2:9).

Once our work here on earth ends, it will continue into heaven but in a new way (because everything is made new). And although we can't know what that will look like, we do know a few differences. For example, although work here on earth can be fulfilling, it can also be frustrating and stressful. But in heaven? All we do will be full of purpose and joy with none of the negative. So what kind of work are we called to do on earth, and how much work do we have to do? Each person is called to something different. Even if you have the exact same job as someone else, you will undoubtedly approach it differently because of your unique giftings. The important thing isn't only the work we do but how we do it. Colossians 3:23 tells us, "Work willingly at whatever you do, as though you were working for the Lord rather than for people." Ecclesiastes 9:10 says, "Whatever you do, do well." These two verses give us all that we need: let's work willingly and well in whatever we are called to do, as though working for the Lord!

However, if we choose to disobey God like Adam and Eve did, our work will often become much harder. What happened when they ate the fruit that God told them not to eat?

First, Adam and Eve wanted to hide from God. Have you ever done this? I know I have. I've made choices or put things before God that cause me to feel shame. Thankfully, we have forgiveness and redemption in Christ when we choose to repent.

Second, Adam and Eve began to blame. We do this too. "I couldn't get my job done because she didn't get hers done" or "I wasn't able to finish because I didn't have all the information I needed." It's so much easier to put the blame on someone else than to accept responsibility ourselves. We are capable of completing what God has put in front of us, and if we aren't, God will equip us! We need to do our jobs, whatever they may be, with integrity.

Disobedience blocks the door to the blessing of hard work. After God discovered the disobedience of Adam and Eve, they were banished from the Garden, had to struggle to eat, and found life painful. But even in that, God made a way. And He makes a way for us. God doesn't claim that our work will be easy, but as long as we put Him first, He will walk with us through it all, guiding, protecting, and blessing the work we set our hands to do.

Everything God does is with intention and purpose. That includes making work part of our spiritual DNA. No matter what we do for work, one job supersedes them all and should always be at the forefront of our life: doing the will of our Father (see John 6:38). For Jesus, that meant dying on the cross to take on the sin of this world and defeating death so we can live eternally with God. That's not our job, but we're still called to die to ourselves and our earthly desires. For us, doing God's will means carrying the torch of the Good News of Jesus—whether in our homes or across the globe. It's so important not to let our jobs here on earth become more important than our heavenly calling. Both are important, but one is eternal. So share God's love as if it's your job. Because it is. Then work with all your heart. Because through that, God is honored.

Let's walk forward into this week viewing work as something we were made to do and not just a means to an end. We can prioritize the job God has placed in front of us by being diligent where He has us and not forgetting why He has us here. As we work hard, blessings will follow. They may not be monetary or even visible, but when we get to heaven, we will see what God was doing through our work all along.

Pray

Dear Lord, thank You for creating me with intention, purpose, and the ability to glorify You through my work. I understand that I am made in Your image and made to work here on this earth. I want to honor You through everything I do. Help me to recognize what unique giftings You've placed inside of me and how those align with the path You've laid out for me. Not only do I want my work to honor You, but I want to use it to share Your love and the gift of eternity with others. Help me to work willingly and with integrity so I'm walking in obedience to You. I don't want to compare myself to others or covet what they have; I just want eternity with You as my treasure and reward. Anything else is extra. Help me to do whatever job You put before me with my whole heart. In Jesus' name, amen.

God is always working, whether we see it or not, and He will answer in His timing.

29

Pray for a Daniel

Don't worry about anything; instead, pray about everything. Tell God what you need, and thank him for all he has done. Then you will experience God's peace, which exceeds anything we can understand. His peace will guard your hearts and minds as you live in Christ Jesus.

PHILIPPIANS 4:6-7

BEFORE I GOT MARRIED or even met my husband, I made a list about the man I hoped I'd marry. But let me give you a little backstory on why and how. I was sitting in a church class, fresh back from a rough experience and environment at college. I found myself in a summer of limbo, wondering if I'd made the right decision to leave school even though, deep down, I knew I had. The Lord blessed me for choosing to leave that environment, but it wasn't exactly smooth sailing. I hit a few bumps and made a few wrong turns but was faithful to seek mentorship and ask God for direction.

Back to the church class. A guest speaker was telling us an emotional story about his daughter, who'd gotten married and had five children only to have her husband leave her. She was devastated. At my young age, I couldn't imagine the specifics of what she was going through, yet I could relate to feeling lost. The speaker continued to share that as his daughter slowly healed, God impressed upon him to pray for her—and not just any prayer. This man felt led to pray specifically that a Boaz would come into his daughter's life and redeem what had been taken from her and her children. If you are unfamiliar with who Boaz is, go read the book of Ruth in the Old Testament. Boaz was what they called a kinsman-redeemer—someone who redeemed a family name through marriage after a husband died. And that's exactly what he did for Ruth. Ruth's story shows that God can take broken, sorrowful circumstances and turn them completely for His glory.

As the speaker wrapped up, I immediately felt a nudge in my heart. Actually, it was less of a nudge and more of a clear command. Ever so softly, I heard the Holy Spirit say, *Pray for a Daniel.* And that was it.

I headed home that night and turned straight to the book of Daniel to read more about the guy I thought I knew all about. Turns out, there was a lot more to him than I'd learned in Sunday school. As I read, I began to write down every quality Daniel possessed. Things like "strong, healthy, and good-looking" (Daniel 1:4) were the obvious ones, but I even wrote down things like "ten times more capable than" others (1:20). I filled two pages with Daniel's amazing qualities. As I sat back and looked at the pages, I thought, *Oh dear, that's a big list to fill.* I mean, I wasn't even half of the things Daniel was, so why should I pray for someone with all of these things to be my husband? Because God told me to. So I did just that. I began to pray for a husband who had these characteristics. Sometimes it felt silly, but I was determined to pray and figured it certainly didn't hurt anything.

Months later, I met a cute guy, and it was love at first sight for both of us. It was as if we just knew that we would end up getting married. When we went on our official first date the next night, we talked about anything and everything. I remember casually asking him, "What's your middle name?" to which he replied "Oh, it's Daniel." My jaw must've dropped to the floor. All those months, all those prayers, and God decided to have a little sense of humor while He was at it. I smiled, and when we were engaged a few months down the road, I told him this story.

As I went back through that journal one night during our engagement, I scanned all the qualities I had been diligently praying for. In both small and big ways, God had answered my prayers. I can look back now and see how some of the Daniel qualities I prayed for have become even more prominent in my husband's life years later.

The easy thing would be to hear this story and think, *Well, all I have to do is make a list and pray, and I'll get what I want.* It may seem like that on the surface, but I want you to look deeper. What is God calling you to pray about—a spouse, a dream, your kids, something else? Are you listening to the nudge of the Holy Spirit and then following it? Are you committing yourself to pray for as long as God calls you to, or are you hoping that things will get better in a day?

I treasure the fact that this will forever be a part of my story. Our story. Not just God's faithfulness but His faithfulness when we are obedient to what He asks of us. *Pray for a Daniel. Make a list.* It was a simple command, but my entire life changed when I was diligent to do so.

Where has God called on you to do something that may have seemed a bit strange at first? God always has a reason, and the more we prioritize our relationship with Him, the more opportunities we have to catch His vision for our lives. Try making a list and praying over it. It might feel funny at first, but God loves to hear our prayers. He is always working, whether we see it or not, and He will answer in His timing.

Let's walk forward into this week asking the Lord if there is an area we should pray over. You might be surprised what He drops on your heart. Commit to praying for that area of life every day for the next week. You might see God answer quickly, or you might need to extend the commitment even longer. No matter how long we pray for something (even a lifetime without an answer), we can trust God that His ways and His timing are always better. No matter what, prayer keeps us in conversation with our heavenly Father, which is always a good thing.

Pray

Dear Lord, thank You that, through the Bible, You've given so many examples of the power of prayer. I want to be better at turning to You in prayer daily so I can deepen my relationship with You. Lord, I need You in every area of my life. I need You to help me discern if there are any areas that need specific prayer right now. If there are, I want to commit to making that happen. Help me, Lord. Please reveal the areas where I can step up and step out, even if it feels uncomfortable at first. Thank You for all the times You have been so faithful even when I haven't been. I want to increase my faithfulness to You. In Jesus' name, amen.

God will be faithful to reply when we learn to recognize and hear His voice.

30

An Open Invitation

When you pray, don't babble on and on as the Gentiles do. They think their prayers are answered merely by repeating their words again and again. Don't be like them, for your Father knows exactly what you need even before you ask him!

MATTHEW 6:7-8

HAVE YOU EVER WANTED TO PRAY, but your prayers felt boring? Or maybe they felt repetitive or uninspired. I've experienced all of these, and I'm convinced of two things. Prayer, no matter how monotonous it feels, always makes a difference when done sincerely. And prayer, no matter how monotonous it feels, opens the door for access to heaven and relationship with God. In that second one, I almost typed "when done sincerely" again, but then I got to thinking about that. Even when done insincerely, prayer still opens the door for talking to God. The difference lies in whether we walk through that door and enter into relationship.

I'll be the first to admit that sometimes I don't know how or what to pray. And that's coming from someone who usually doesn't lack words. I'm extra thankful that, even when I don't know how to pray, God knows exactly what I need before I ask Him. However, this doesn't get me off the hook. Just because God knows everything doesn't mean we don't say anything. Conversations require two participants, and we are one of those! Thankfully, Scripture gives us helpful insight when we are at a loss for how to pray.

First, God has given us the Holy Spirit as our Helper and Advocate. In Romans 8:26-27, we read, "The Holy Spirit helps us in our weakness. For example, we don't know what God wants us to pray for. But the Holy Spirit prays for us with groanings that cannot be expressed in words. And the Father who knows all hearts knows what the Spirit is saying, for the Spirit pleads for us believers in harmony with God's own will." I love how even when we don't have words, the Holy Spirit helps us pray, and the Father responds! Isn't that great? As believers, we should all be consistently inviting the Holy Spirit to be active in our lives.

Second, Jesus modeled a way for us to pray. In Luke 11, a disciple asked Jesus to teach them how to pray. This is what Jesus says in verses 2-4: "This is how you should pray: 'Father, may your name be kept holy. May your Kingdom come soon. Give us each day the food we need, and forgive us our sins, as we forgive those who sin against us. And don't let us yield to temptation." Did you notice how Jesus prayed boldly here? We can do that too. He didn't use fancy words or long-winded poetry, but He did follow a pattern. He honored God's name, recognized His power, and sought His will first, and then He asked for His basic needs (nothing more), asked for forgiveness, and finally asked for protection from temptation. When we know nothing else to pray, we can pray this with all our heart, knowing that God is pleased to hear us call out to Him. Isn't that great?

Prayer isn't for God; it's a gift *from* God for us to be in communication with Him. Consider it an open invitation to talk with your best friend whenever you need to. Because it's not just asking for things constantly. It's crying out, praising, thanking God, and honoring Him for all He's done and is going to do. We need to be a people that prays in all circumstances and without ceasing. Why? Because the more we pray, the more opportunities we have to hear from God.

I mentioned earlier that prayer opens the door to heaven. Well, doors work both ways. God loves to speak to us the same way we speak to Him. So as we pray, let's take the time to listen for the Lord's response. He will be faithful to reply when we learn to recognize and hear His voice.

A few verses after Jesus teaches His disciples how to pray, He says, "And so I tell you, keep on asking, and you will receive what you ask for. Keep on seeking, and you will find. Keep on knocking, and the door will be opened to you. For everyone who asks, receives. Everyone who seeks, finds. And to everyone who knocks, the door will be opened" (Luke 11:9-10). What a promise and call to not let prayer be a one-time thing but a lifelong response of thankfulness.

Let's walk forward into this week being intentional not just to pray and repeat words but to seek God in our prayers. Find a time each day this week to follow the pattern Jesus laid out for us: recognize God's holiness, ask for our daily needs, ask for forgiveness of any sin and extend that same forgiveness to others, and thank Him for His protection over your life. Then give God room to speak, and listen for His voice. The power of prayer is guaranteed to transform your life.

Pray

Dear Lord, today I want to pray just like Jesus taught His disciples—because I am also one of His disciples. Father, may Your name be kept holy. May Your Kingdom come soon. Thank You that I can honor Your name. Build me up to live in Your will, Lord. To live with an expectancy of Your Kingdom coming. Second, I pray that You would give me the food I need each day. I thank You that You give me exactly what I need. Not just food but everything. What You give is always good, and there's purpose to Your plans. Help me to see that. Third, please forgive my sins as I forgive those who sin against me. Help me to recognize sin in my own life and repent of it immediately so I don't continue to walk in disobedience. What a gift it is to be forgiven, Lord. I pray that I would extend the same grace that You have extended to me. Finally, don't let me yield to temptation. Thank You that You give me an out in every situation. Help me to choose Your way, which is always the best way. Give me strength to keep away from those things that aren't honoring to You. In Jesus' name, amen.

Within the boundaries God establishes for our good, we find true freedom.

31

The Right Environment

Don't be fooled by those who say such things,
for "bad company corrupts good character."

1 CORINTHIANS 15:33

WITH THE HELP OF MY PARENTS, I spent hours upon hours my junior and senior years sending out letters and videos to various colleges in hopes that one of them would recruit me to play softball. It was my yearslong dream, and I had worked so hard for it. Midpoint of my senior year, I was invited on two college visits and was so excited. We were only able to afford one plane ticket, so I went without my parents. Let me tell you, flying across the country to a college all by yourself for the first time is quite the adventure, and that's before you add negotiating potential scholarships. After these visits, I was humbled to receive a pretty decent scholarship offer from both colleges. I ultimately picked the college I felt the Lord gave me the most peace about. It was in Michigan, over half a country away from where I called home. I was equal parts excited and scared to take on such an adventure.

After moving all my stuff into the dorm (this time with my mom there to help), we waved one last goodbye, and I sobbed like a baby as she headed back to the airport. I knew that no matter what happened, I was at least a $450 plane ticket and thousands of miles from home. But I was confident that everything would be just wonderful. And at first, it was. There was so much to discover. Being part of a team was also fun, and I was eager to befriend my teammates. As the months went on, though, the initial excitement wore off and I began to have a clearer perspective of the college environment, and it wasn't what I'd hoped it would be. In fact, it was terrible.

Early in the semester, I was invited by a teammate to come hang out with some other athletes. Once I arrived, I quickly realized that it was more than just a casual hangout—it was turning into a party that I wasn't interested in staying for. I asked for a ride back to my dorm. On the way there, she told me, "You'll get used to it," to which I replied, "I don't really want to." And that was the beginning of the end. The more I said no to various parties, bad decision-making, and questionable ways of living, the more isolated I became. I had to work to find a church and seek out relationships with like-minded young adults just so I wouldn't get too lonely.

After my freshman year, I went home and felt like I could breathe again. It was so refreshing and refilled my cup to the point that as I prepped for my sophomore year, it once again seemed doable. I reminded myself of my original dream and returned to college feeling hopeful. I promised myself that, no matter what anyone else chose to do, I could make right choices. But the same things began to happen, and I felt so alone. I knew I couldn't stand it much longer. It wasn't worth any amount of scholarship money to be in an environment filled with overtly sinful choices.

The devil is out to "steal and kill and destroy" (John 10:10), and that's not an exaggeration. But we can play offense and combat the enemy with God's power inside us. How can we do that? By intentionally choosing the right environment and surrounding ourselves with good influences. Daily. That might sound extreme, but living life for Jesus is worth it because eternity is worth it. There is a reason God gives us guidelines to live by: He knows what happens outside those guidelines. The world calls it freedom, but that type of freedom makes you a slave to the cycle of sin—and sin beats you down over and over, requiring you to give more of yourself and your values in order to stay "relevant." Within the boundaries God establishes for our good, we find true freedom.

The influence of others affects everything: how we act, what we do, and when and how we do it. The good news is we have a choice. If you're in the middle of an environment that's not good for you, go find a better one. Even if it hurts. The temporary pain will be eclipsed by what the Lord has for you as you walk in His freedom.

After my sophomore year, I left for good. I gave up a scholarship and a lifelong dream and decided that I would rather follow whatever dream the Lord had for me. That summer, I got a call from my former coach offering me even more scholarship money to come back. One hundred percent coverage. Something I had always hoped for. For a split second, it sounded tempting. But thinking about the environment made it an easy "No, thank you!" Money was temporary. My relationship with the Lord is eternal, and that's not worth compromising no matter how solid in your faith you think you are.

Want to hear the cool part? One year after coming home, I met my husband, Tim, got accepted to nursing school (my other dream), and deepened my relationship with the Lord. Not only that, but one of my former teammates, who I hadn't even been that close with at the time, stayed in touch with me. Through a series of events that only God could orchestrate, she moved to my hometown to also leave the environment I had been in, became such a close friend, and was quickly "adopted" as a part of our family (and more importantly, a part of God's family!). Even in hindsight, I wouldn't want to change anything about my experiences because I learned from them and grew in my giftings with the Lord. But hindsight also helps me know I won't take an opportunity in an environment like that again, no matter how much I'm tempted. I can't always avoid the world and people's choices in it, but I can make intentional choices for myself that create an atmosphere honoring to the Lord.

Let's walk forward into this week examining the environment we're living in and ask the Lord how we can make a shift for the better. Let's not miss out on God because we are trying not to miss out on the world.

Pray

Dear Lord, thank You that You have good purposes and plans for me. And You want me to help create an atmosphere that shines for You. I know I can't avoid all the things of the world, but I ask that You infuse Yourself in and through me so I shine Your light wherever I go. Help me prayerfully consider decisions I make that would affect who and what is around me. I ask that when I find myself in a situation that is less than I'd hoped for, You would either make a way out or guide me through it. Lord, let it be my main goal to be salt and light to a dark world. Help me start right where I am to brighten the corners of my own life so I can impact others for Your Kingdom. In Jesus' name, amen.

God has plenty to teach us, no matter how much we're capable of in our current season.

32

With All Your Heart

Work willingly at whatever you do, as though you were working for the Lord rather than for people. Remember that the Lord will give you an inheritance as your reward, and that the Master you are serving is Christ.

COLOSSIANS 3:23–24

AS I WAS DRIVING AROUND with our kids delivering May Day flowers, I had a thought. *I wish I was more consistent doing these types of things.* Have you ever felt that way? Wanting to do more or wishing you could be more consistent with certain traditions or special days—especially when you see others doing more than you are? But what even is "more"? In reality, it's usually just a standard we've made up in our heads that keeps us trapped in a game of comparison. The reality is that we don't have to do it all; nor can we. Nor do we have to always do something we've always done just for the sake of keeping it up or keeping the tradition alive.

Probably two or three years ago, I came to a point in motherhood (and life) where I realized it was okay to do the things I could do in each season and not hold myself to a standard of doing it all the time. If it worked out one year to deliver flowers on May Day, great! If it didn't work out the next year, that's okay too. Finding the freedom to let go of comparisons and the expectations we place on ourselves is such a gift from the Lord. He gives us peace to rest in what He has made us able to do. Does this mean we should never do anything? Not at all. But it does allow us to lean into what God has placed before us each day and not force certain things just for the sake of keeping up with others.

I love traditions. Most of all, I love Christmas traditions. Everything from decorating to doing all the festivities brings me such joy. But I remember one Christmas where nothing seemed to come together. First it was the decorations.

I looked at what I had and felt bummed that I didn't have time to get it all up. Then I visited my mom's house and saw all her sweet little areas that brought me so much joy and realized that I wanted my house to look like that. I even casually said something out loud, and my mom stopped me in my tracks.

"Sarah, I'm in a completely different season than you. I don't have any little children running around or babies crawling and grabbing decorations. I can do this now, but there was a time I couldn't. And you are in that time."

I immediately felt ridiculous for comparing myself to my mom, who is thirty-one years older. I mean, it's one thing to compare myself to my peers. But my mom? It was absurd, but that just goes to show you how quickly comparison can creep up in our minds.

Seasons are seasons for a reason. They ebb and flow, and they don't last forever. If they did, life would surely be boring. Instead, we are made to grow, and what we learn in each season grows us for what's next. For many, the season of parenting is a precursor to the season of grandparenting. My mom would say she is a way better grandparent than she was a parent because God nurtured specific things in her during her parenting years that are just now coming to fruition. Things that felt hard then feel doable now.

Some seasons I'm able to make meals for groups of people, while others I'm knee-deep in diapers and just trying to get meals together for my own family. Some seasons I find I can run more errands in town, while others I'm stuck at home with multiple naptimes. One isn't better than the other. God has plenty to teach us, no matter how much we're capable of in our current season.

Whatever season we are in, God calls us to do exactly what our verse this week says: to work with a willing heart at whatever is placed before us *and* to do it for the Lord. He's the One we are aiming to please, and when that happens, what we are called to do won't seem like a burden. God isn't going to call you to something because He wants to weigh you down and make your week harder. God is going to call you to something because it will bring growth that will propel and carry you into your next season. God is going to call you to something because He wants to prune and bring new growth into that area of your life. He cares enough about us not to leave us stuck in a season without purpose.

Here's the takeaway: whatever the Lord has put before you to do, do it with *all your heart*! Do it with joy! It's the heart and motivations behind what we do that matters. And God gives us grace for the different seasons we walk through.

Let's step forward into this week taking a look at what's around us and how we can embrace the season God has called us to. Is there an expectation from a previous season that we need to let go of so we can move into what God has for us? If so, we can release it to Him and ask Him to give us the strength we need to face whatever is next. In all things, let's choose to work willingly at what we can with a heart after God and not a heart of comparison!

Pray

Dear Lord, I'm so thankful for all I have. Throughout my life You've given me everything I need and more. In every season You've walked with me through, I've never lacked. You continue to faithfully show me the areas You've called me to, and You equip me for each and every one. Lord, help me to keep my eyes on You and not on others as I do what You've called me to do. Forgive me for the times I've let expectations and comparisons get in the way of what You have for me. I want to let go of what I think I need to do and exchange it for Your perspective in my life. Align my heart with Yours in each and every season I walk through. And, Lord, as I set myself to do whatever You've placed before me, I want to do it willingly. Don't let me grow weary of doing Your work because I know that it will reap a harvest that impacts the Kingdom of Heaven. I'm willing, Lord. Use me! In Jesus' name, amen.

It's never too late to ask the Lord to strengthen and establish your identity.

33

God-Given Identity

You are not like that, for you are a chosen people. You are royal priests, a holy nation, God's very own possession. As a result, you can show others the goodness of God, for he called you out of the darkness into his wonderful light.

1 PETER 2:9

ONE OF THE BEST THINGS we can do for our children is speak life over them and help call out their God-given identity from an early age. We live in a world that is fighting to control the identity of children. As parents, it is imperative that we do our part to protect who God has made them to be. This begins at home! When I was growing up, my parents would talk a lot about how we all have different giftings and "bents." For some, that may be something creative or artsy, for others it might be something athletic, and for others it might be something with building or engineering. There are endless possibilities, and it's no secret that there are lots of talented people in our world. But talent will only take you so far and won't fill the places that are meant to be filled by God. When people know *who they are* and not just *what they can do*, it changes how they use their talents, and it has the potential for eternal impact in God's Kingdom.

As parents, we have the incredible opportunity to ask the Lord to help us build *His identity* into our children. We can pray and ask the Lord to help us see what giftings they have from a young age. We can also just pay attention and see where they thrive and what causes them to want to learn new things. For example, one of our sons loves to build. Whether magnetic tiles, Legos, train sets, or anything else, he is naturally detail-oriented and will take the time to build elaborate constructions that I can't even imagine doing myself. To top it all off, he exhibits patience, gentleness, and self-control.

As my son grows, I'm going to take the time to specifically compliment him in those areas I mentioned. I'm going to tell him what a great job he does building things. But I'm also going to tell him that I see the spiritual component of that gift as well. That, along with building physical structures in a practical sense, he can be a builder of community and relationships—and more specifically a builder of God's Kingdom. I want him to know this so well that even when he misses the mark, he will walk away unshaken in his purpose and calling. Because I've reminded him of it over and over. Because I've spoken words of life over him for so many years. Because I've told him who he is in Jesus countless times. I want my kids to know that no mistake changes their identity in Christ. That's set in stone.

From about nine to noon, we work on our homeschool lessons. My mom and I talk almost every day, and she tries to avoid calling me during homeschool so we don't get distracted (because when Nana calls, we all want to visit with her!).

But one school day, she happened to call. Her first question was "How is your day going?" and to her surprise my answer wasn't good. I actually started crying but managed to say we were having a tough day all around. My teaching, my kids' learning, all our emotions—nothing was working like I hoped. Mom reminded me that this was one day out of lots of days, and this one day didn't change the type of mother I am or how effective I am in teaching my kids. It was just a less-than day. I could choose to shake it off and approach the next day brand-new.

Maybe you need this type of readjustment too. Maybe when you were growing up, no one ever took the time to help you establish your identity in Christ. Or maybe you did learn about your identity in Christ, but as you grew and launched into the world, that identity was beaten down to the point where you've forgotten who God made you to be. Be encouraged that it's never too late to ask the Lord to strengthen and establish your identity.

As a mom, sometimes I feel like all I do is parent, and that's all I'll ever do. When my kids were younger, sometimes I felt like outside of pregnancy and having a baby in my arms, I wasn't sure what to do with myself. If I wasn't pregnant or didn't have a baby, did I still have a purpose? Absolutely. Because no matter what season I'm in, who I am in Christ never changes. My kids will get older, and I may change how I parent, but my identity does not change. Celebrate each season you are in, cultivate it, and get everything you can from it. But also know that our God always has more for us because our identity isn't tied to one accomplishment or area. God is a big-picture God, and each season gives us something that will equip us for whatever He is calling us to next.

Let's walk forward into this week asking the Lord to help us recognize at least one God-given identity quality in each of our children that we can begin calling out and speaking life over. And let's ask the Lord to remind us of our God-given giftings and bents that make up who we are in Christ.

Pray

Dear Lord, thank You that You made no mistakes when You made me and that You give me exactly what I need and remind me of exactly who I am in You. I pray that You would begin to show me who You created my children to be. Give me glimpses of their natural giftings and bents, and help me to speak life over them as much as possible. God, I want to drench them in Your love so they never forget it. I want them to know that when things don't go well, they can still turn to You and stand solidly in who they are. Lord, I also ask You to remind me of my identity in You. I don't want to get so wrapped up in what I'm doing that I forget who I am. Help me to be the mother, wife, daughter, sister, and friend You made me to be. Your will first, Lord. In Jesus' name, amen.

When we are in a season of need, God calls on other people to pour into us the way we pour into them.

34

Build Each Other Up

Let us think of ways to motivate one another
to acts of love and good works.

HEBREWS 10:24

MY MOM IS THE BEST at encouraging others. I am always so amazed at how she intentionally thinks of someone, decides on how she can best encourage them, and then follows through. Whether it's a card, a treat, a little gift, or one-on-one quality time, she makes people feel so seen and loved right where they are. I could share countless stories of women who told me, "I remember when your mom did [fill in the blank] for me, and it was right when I needed it." What a gift to have!

Encouragement is something I'm working on in my own life. It takes effort and practice, but encouraging others is something we can *all* do. It's not just for the people who are "natural encouragers." Why? Because different people need different people who can provide different types of encouragement. The way I make someone feel loved won't be the same way you make someone feel loved.

But it's not a competition. We can all work together to encourage and build one another up. This isn't just a good idea—it's a biblical command. First Thessalonians 5:11 calls us to "encourage each other and build each other up, just as you are already doing." I used to think that obeying this command would cost me a lot of time and money, but I've realized that is not true at all. Sending a text is free. Mailing a card costs as much as a stamp. Making double of the meal you planned for dinner doesn't add too much expense or time. We can work with what we have, where we are.

Next, we can start to become attentive to those around us, looking for opportunities to encourage someone right where they are at. Do you know a friend who is having a particularly hard week? Someone who is suffering a loss? A mom who's doing a great job? We don't have to wait for the perfect moment to offer encouragement. We just need to pay attention to others, which is always a good practice.

A while back, our church held a weeklong time of prayer where everyone signed up and committed to pray for an hour at the church. The goal was to have at least one person praying day and night for the whole week. They set up a room with different stations to pray for different needs and spend time with the Lord in a peaceful environment. When it was our turn, Tim was out of town, so I ended up having to take the kids all by myself. An hour of "quiet and peaceful" prayer time with seven kids in the room wasn't exactly relaxing, but it ended up being a special time for us to share. One of the stations was an area where you could write cards to someone the Lord put on your heart to encourage. As I sat there, a friend immediately came to mind. I really felt like the Lord gave me a specific encouragement to share with her. So I wrote my note, tucked it in my diaper bag, and we went home for the day.

Months later, I was digging through my diaper bag, and lo and behold—at the very bottom was that note I had written for my friend. I was so bummed when I saw it. I had totally meant to send it when I wrote it because I felt like it was a specific encouragement just for her. Now what? I decided that even though I was sending it late, God could still use it to encourage my friend. Because it's not about my timing. God's timing is always right and always perfect, and He can (thankfully) work through our forgetfulness to have an impact on people's hearts. So I placed the letter in the mail, trusting the Lord to do what He does best.

A couple of weeks went by, and I didn't think about that letter again. Then a knock came on my door. I went to open it and who was there? The friend I had sent the card to. We greeted with a giant hug since we hadn't seen each other in a while and as we hugged she said, "You have no idea how much I needed your card this week and how much it blessed me." Wow! Only the Lord could have done that. She handed me a loaf of homemade sourdough bread with a note of thanks, and after we visited for a bit, she headed home. It was so life-giving. That card blessed her, but her visit blessed me (and the loaf of bread was excitedly devoured by our family). That's not why we do it, but that's just how kind God is. When we are in a season of need, God calls on other people to pour back into us the way we pour into them.

I love how the Lord works that way. We think we are doing one thing, but in reality there is so much more happening in our hearts and in heaven. Things we see but also things only God sees. We may never know the impact or ripple effect of a single encouraging action, but I can tell you this: none of it is in vain. When we do our part, we know we are walking in obedience to God's calling *and* we get to be part of His purposes. It requires effort, but none of it will be left unnoticed—at least in God's eyes. We can do this, friend. We can take simple actions to make a difference in others' days and weeks. We can pay attention to those around us and find ways to make them feel loved and seen. We can each use the ways God has gifted us to love others. And we can do all of this starting now!

Let's walk forward into this week thinking of one person we can encourage or show extra kindness to. Think of whether you can send an encouraging text, drop by for a hug, bake something, or anything else! Whatever it is, even though you are the one doing the action, trust that you are also partnering with the Lord and He will make the encouragement go further than you could on your own.

Pray

Dear Lord, thank You for being the God who encourages me and never leaves or forsakes me when I'm not at my best. Help me to see the needs around me. I can use what You've given me to make a positive impact on others, whether friends and family, acquaintances, or even strangers. I want to do my part and take action so people see Your love through me and want that love in their lives too. Lord, help me not to get overwhelmed but to start where I am and with what I have. I recognize that You've uniquely gifted me to help and bless others, so I want to do just that. In Jesus' name, amen.

God will continue doing the good work He started in us.

35

The Power of Self-Control

A person without self-control is like a city with broken-down walls.

PROVERBS 25:28

"WHO DO WE CONTROL?"

At this point, my kids know the answer to that question by heart. "We control ourselves and what we can."

With seven kids, you probably can imagine that not everyone gets along all the time. Sometimes my kids react unkindly to one another, and discipline has to happen. Most of the time, the conflict and its consequences wouldn't have happened if everyone had used self-control and good communication. But our kids are growing and learning, so no matter what, after everyone is calm, we all get to have a good conversation about what it looks like to control our reactions to others.

You know, sometimes it's not even the kids who struggle with this the most. As adults, we have been known to behave in similar ways. After all, where did our kids learn this behavior? Sure, some of it is built into us, but a lot of it is modeled for us. We learn by observing. And learning the hard way can often be . . . well, hard! But based on what the Bible says about it, self-control is one of the keys to living at peace with one another as God calls us to (see Romans 12:18). Imagine if everyone had automatic self-control in everything. It would eliminate so much sin, so many poor decisions, and so much discipline. Instead, we might see wisdom behind every decision, people holding themselves to a higher standard, and productive, healthy conversations. Self-control has the power to change our life, our community, and our world.

I think the metaphor in Proverbs 25:28 is such a good visual of why self-control is important. Can you imagine a city with a giant wall around it? That's us. Every time we lose our self-control, whether a little or a lot, it chips away at our walls. Slowly but surely, the strength of the walls diminishes. Slowly but surely, our ability to handle things in a God-honoring way diminishes. And as you can probably guess, slowly but surely this begins to affect every area of our lives. It may not seem like much when you just look at each isolated incident, but when you put them all together, it's a recipe for disaster.

I was listening to a talk at a homeschooling conference one time, and the speaker said something that really intrigued me. She said if your child feels like they can't do something, they won't try. So as parents, we need to remind them of what they can do by reminding them of a time when they actually did it. Let's take a math test, for example. Instead of saying "C'mon, honey, you can do it. I know you can," we could instead say something like "Remember last week when you didn't think you could get more than half the math problems right, but you actually got 16 out of 20 correct? You did it then, so I know you can do it again." This sort of encouraging reminder can change their mindset from negative to positive. It trains their brain, which is such a healthy help starting at a young age. We can apply this to self-control to train kids that they can control their actions when and how they want to because we've seen them do it before.

Guess what? This approach isn't just for children. I've been practicing this kind of self-talk in my own life because self-control was something I consistently struggled with in the early years of my marriage—and it remains a challenge even now. But with God's help, I've gotten so much better. I'm rebuilding the wall that I slowly chipped away. It's stronger than ever now, as God reminds me of what I have done with His help and how I can continue growing in this area.

Self-control is the key to a lot of other difficulties we may be facing in our life. How we respond and how we handle ourselves in less-than-ideal conditions or conversations can make all the difference. How we model self-control and how we implement it during difficult conversations and interactions can not only change our heart and habits but also turn the hearts of others toward the Lord. We control ourselves and allow God to do the rest. Honestly, that's a relief for me. I don't have to do God's job or anyone else's. Hallelujah!

Let's walk forward into this week recognizing any areas where we may need to ask for forgiveness for our lack of self-control. Let's give that to God and ask Him to step in, give us wisdom, and help us flourish in all areas of our lives. He will continue doing the good work He started in us.

Pray

Dear Lord, I'm asking for Your help with self-control because I don't want to be controlled by whatever I feel in the moment. I don't want my feelings to be the driving factor behind my interactions with others or how I manage myself. You want me to live a disciplined life, Lord, and I know that takes work. Will You help me find ways I can grow in this? When I fall short, help me to be quick to ask for forgiveness and to see how I can do better next time. Teach me to stop, think, and pray before I react. Help me to choose the right response and reaction instead of living on impulse. Thank You for caring about me in this way, Lord. I want to honor You in everything I do. In Jesus' name, amen.

There is no
sweeter music
to God's ears
than repentance.

36

Clean Out Your Heart

Create in me a clean heart, O God.
Renew a loyal spirit within me.

PSALM 51:10

TWICE A YEAR, I spend at least a couple of days sorting through bins and bins of clothes to exchange the kids' summer clothes for their fall and winter wardrobes. Then vice versa six months later. Not to mention the in-between times when one child grows two inches in two months and suddenly those pants I bought for the new school year need to be passed down to a younger brother. (Thankfully, with six boys in a row, we've been able to get our money's worth out of our clothes as they've passed from one brother to another.) I've done this routine so many times over the years. Lay ten or so bins out, and rotate sizes and seasons for each boy. When I tell you it's a task, I mean it.

One time in particular, as I was folding/moving/sorting, I felt like the Lord ever so gently spoke this to me: *Sarah, just as you are cleaning out the boys' closets and clothes, sorting through and getting rid of pieces with stains and holes, and putting new sizes in, I want to do that same thing inside of you and your heart.* It was as quick as it was subtle, and it felt like a loving gift from God. I knew cleaning out my heart might not feel good, but I want to listen to whatever God has to say to me.

Whenever I sort through clothes, I have certain rules for what I keep and don't keep. I do this because my personality wants to keep everything. Whether there's a sentimental story behind it or a reason why it can still be used despite being in awful shape, I have a really hard time letting go. So I had to set rules. Anything with holes or tears has to go. Anything that has more than one stain that can't be removed has to go. Anything that has faded or yellowed—gone! As you can imagine, if I didn't follow my own rules, I would be a clothes hoarder for every size from newborn on up.

Isn't that a good metaphor for our hearts? I know that, over time, just like my boys' closets, my heart gets cluttered. Some areas become tattered and torn. Some areas get stains from sin or unforgiveness. Other areas have lost their luster because I haven't tended to them. If I leave my heart in this condition, I will become a hoarder of unhealthy baggage. I'll continue carrying around frustration, trauma, and sin instead of allowing the Lord to replace those areas with fresh growth and His goodness. And just as I take certain steps to trade out my boys' clothes, we can take steps to clean out our hearts.

First, we have to invite God to enter our lives. This is the most important thing. You might know that it's going to hurt when He cleans out certain areas and asks you to sacrifice things you've held on to for so long. But here's another perspective: if you know it's going to hurt, then you probably already know it isn't something that's in your best interest to hang on to. It's just hard to let go. Usually, we have an inkling of the things that aren't right for us. We often fight to keep them, but our moral compass lets us know better. Lean into that inkling (because really it's a nudging of the Holy Spirit). Welcome God with both arms and your whole heart.

Second, we have to let God see the deepest, most vulnerable parts of our heart so He can heal and clean them out. That's hard, I know. Nobody wants somebody knowing their dirty laundry—aka sin. But here's the good news: God already knows. Because He created you, He knows you inside and out whether you like it or not. So those deep, dark, hard spots aren't hard for God. He has already made a way for you to be forgiven. We need to let the Lord bring those things to light so He can show us how He has already defeated them.

Finally, we need to have a repentant heart. One that says, *I'm so sorry for the yucky parts of my life that have caused me to sin and be separated from You. Please forgive me for not letting You in. Create in me a clean heart, O God, and take the place of every sinful thing in my life.* There is no sweeter music to God's ears than repentance. He loves it and forgives us freely when we ask.

When we welcome God in, allow Him to see us for who we are, and ask Him to clean out our hearts, we can walk in the second half of our verse this week: "Renew a loyal spirit within me." Once the spirit of darkness is gone, we need a 180-degree turn along with a new set of clothes from Christ. We can ask the Holy Spirit to help our spirit reflect His. We can ask Him to fill us with right thinking and right attitudes. As I sit there each season and look at the pile of old, damaged clothes I'm letting go of, I'm reminded to let the Lord do the same thing in my heart. I don't want to hold on too tightly to things that are worn out or stained with sin. Instead, I want to walk in newness with Christ.

Let's walk forward into this week opening our hearts to the Lord for a cleanout. If you've been holding on to some sinful patterns or tendencies that are taking up God's space in your life, say them out loud and ask God to help you repent and replace them with what He has for you! I guarantee He has something waiting that's so much better.

Pray

Dear Lord, I need You to clean out my heart. I've been unwilling to let go of some sins and shameful areas of my life because it feels too vulnerable to let anyone in—even You. But I know I need a heart change, and I know You can do that for me. Be gentle but firm as You expose the areas that need to be moved out of my life. I ask Your forgiveness for all those areas. Thank You that You died on the cross, carrying my sin so I don't have to. Please replace that sin with Your purposes for my life. Give me a heart that is soft and ready for what You will call me to. May everything I do be a reflection of what You've done in my life. In Jesus' name, amen.

Our main qualification isn't physical power but integrity.

37

Be a Gatekeeper

Joyful are people of integrity,
who follow the instructions of the LORD.

PSALM 119:1

THE BIBLE TELLS US that people who have integrity "do not compromise with evil" (Psalm 119:3). I love the power in that statement. There is no in-between option where we can allow a little evil in. Forgetaboutit. Evil is evil. We are called to be gatekeepers for all aspects of our lives, our families, and our homes. We must be alert to the schemes of the enemy so we aren't caught off guard.

You've probably seen gatekeepers in movies. Usually they are strong warriors who carry some sort of massive weapon and wear a big helmet. Often they have special abilities to see what's coming from afar so they can warn others of potential danger. But even though the movies depict them as people of great strength and stature, being a gatekeeper of our life is something we are all called to do whether or not we feel qualified. The main qualification isn't physical power but integrity.

My dad (affectionately called Papa most of the time these days) had a career as an engineer. No, not the kind that works with wires, draws up blueprints, or designs bridges. I'm talking about the kind that drives big trains. A train engineer. I always thought he had the coolest job. "My dad drives trains!" You just don't hear that much, do you?

My dad tells me that driving a train was a career with a rough crowd. These men and women worked hard, got little rest, operated in tight quarters, slept in hotels more often than at home, and spent long hours on a train. Not ideal, but he said you really got to know a person on a train. Their true self. And one of the things that came out in many conversations was a lack of integrity—in marriages, parenting, communication, and more. Many of the conversations he heard were less than edifying. So he decided to devote himself to being a person of integrity in everything he said and did. It wasn't easy, but most worthwhile things in life aren't easy. I can say with confidence that my dad is one of the people in my life with the most integrity. No matter what people say of him, to him, or behind his back, he never wavers in his commitment to honor the Lord in everything he does.

He also spent forty-plus years driving engines all around and sacrificing a lot of sleep. When you are a train engineer, your trips can last over twenty-four hours. Once you get home, you don't have much time for sleep before they can call you back in. The problem was that when my dad was home, he wanted to see his children. Sleep became a second thought for him. As we grew older, he knew he wanted a way to see us more, so he opened a construction business. As he thought about what to call it, the name Integrity Builders came to mind. To this day, I can't think of a more fitting name for my dad's business than one with the word *integrity* in it. Despite mistakes and learning curves, my dad always did everything with integrity—even when he didn't gain from it.

When I married my husband, Tim, I knew he was also an incredible man of integrity. I was given advice early in our marriage to ask the Lord how I could pray for my husband. That day, I was reading Proverbs 10, and I felt led to pray verse 9 over Tim: "People with integrity walk safely, but those who follow crooked paths will be exposed." Having integrity is something the enemy hates. He will throw everything he can to make someone stumble in that area. Which is why having integrity and being a gatekeeper go hand in hand. To have integrity, you *must* be a gatekeeper as well. For your mind, your family, your home, your work, everything! It's important to be on guard at all times against the schemes of the enemy.

Thankfully, we don't have to be gatekeepers under our own strength. If you're a follower of Christ, you automatically have the armor of God, which allows us to fight the enemy with God's truth. (Check out Ephesians 6:13-18). The Lord equips us with discernment and wisdom as we strive to defend our lives from evil.

And we understand that our battle isn't "against flesh-and-blood enemies." Our battle is "against evil rulers and authorities of the unseen world" (Ephesians 6:12).

This should fire us up! In Christ, we have everything we need to live a life of integrity. We have all the wisdom we need to block the devil's schemes before he even gets a chance to put them in play. We are prepared for spiritual battle because we know who we're really fighting. Let's choose to stay on course and stay alert so that we are walking in obedience to God's commands. By living with integrity and choosing to be a gatekeeper, we can do just that. And the reward goes far beyond benefits here on earth.

As we walk forward into this week, let's walk in integrity and only let right and good and godly things be a part of who we are and what we take in. If you are facing a situation that isn't of the Lord and has caused compromise in your life, confess it, repent of it, and ask God to help you live with integrity in all you do.

Pray

Dear Lord, thank You that I don't fight my battles on my own. I willingly put on the armor of God to help me be a warrior for You and to battle any sin that might try to make its way into my heart and mind. Lord, I want to be a gatekeeper for my life and my home. Help me to walk in integrity in everything I say and do so that nothing can be held against me. You've equipped me for all You've called me to do, and I choose to walk in that each day. Help me understand what it means to walk in obedience to Your commands so others see a reflection of You in my life. In Jesus' name, amen.

God is calling you, right where you are at, to choose today whom you will serve.

38

A Lasting Legacy

We will not hide these truths from our children; we will tell the next generation about the glorious deeds of the LORD, about his power and his mighty wonders.

PSALM 78:4

OFTEN I THINK ON HOW THANKFUL I am for the gift of legacy—not just on my side of the family but in my husband's extended family as well. My parents have worked hard to foster a sense of belonging, tradition, and pride in our family all the while acknowledging everything the Lord has done for us. Tim's parents have done the same. I realize not everyone has that kind of heritage, but I think one of the coolest aspects of any of our lives is that we can choose to start fresh and begin a turning point for ourselves that will affect everyone who comes after us.

My grandpa tells the story of how when he met my grandma, she was engaged to someone else. But that didn't stop him. After their first meeting, Grandma ended up breaking off the engagement, falling in love with my grandpa, and marrying him. My grandma came from a family of alcoholics, while my grandpa came from a family that was raised pretty strictly and knew the Lord. From the beginning, they chose to start serving the Lord together. That decision changed the lives of everyone after them, me and our children included.

My grandparents soon decided they wanted to start a family, and shortly after Grandpa got back from serving in the military, Grandma gave birth to my dad. After that, they couldn't get pregnant again for years. So they stopped trying and settled on the fact that they may only have one child. Twelve years later, though, they had another baby—my aunt! Those two kids grew up and started families of their own. From them came seven grandkids (one of whom is in heaven). From all of us grandkids came twenty-nine grandkids. Forty-nine people total in their legacy so far.

Isn't that incredible? If you think so, I'll tell you something even more incredible. Every single person in our family is serving the Lord. Not because we know it all, but because we've all made our own choice to follow the God who does. Has it always been easy? No. Have we always made the right decisions? No. But every day, we try to make intentional decisions to follow the Lord, obey what He calls us to do, and pass on my grandparents' heritage of faithfulness. The Lord's work in the hearts of two people—as well as their continuing obedience—created a legacy not just here on earth but in heaven as well. And that's just one part of our family history. I could tell many similar stories from Tim's side as well.

Now imagine with me for a moment how many people have been and will be impacted for the Lord from any family choosing Christ as their foundation. Families can focus on a lot of different things, but impacting people's lives for eternity is the greatest of them all, don't you think? Although it doesn't guarantee that everyone will follow God's plan for their life, building your family on the foundation of the Lord is the best choice you can make.

In my head, I picture legacy as a tree. One person chooses to plant themselves. The tree starts growing, and its roots go deep. Soon, branches extend, and the branches sprout leaves, and the tree continues to grow! But that first step is what feeds the rest of the tree and creates the legacy. If you don't have a godly legacy in your family, start today and plant yourself. Make a choice to say, "I'm going to do it differently." Don't let the fear and the overwhelm of where you've come from keep you from choosing differently for yourself, your family, and the future. God's promises follow those who follow Him.

In the book of Joshua, chapter 24, Joshua reminds the Israelites of all God did for them and how He brought them through. In verses 14-15, he says,

> So fear the LORD and serve him wholeheartedly. Put away forever the idols your ancestors worshiped when they lived beyond the Euphrates River and

in Egypt. Serve the LORD alone. But if you refuse to serve the LORD, then choose today whom you will serve. Would you prefer the gods your ancestors served beyond the Euphrates? Or will it be the gods of the Amorites in whose land you now live? But as for me and my family, we will serve the LORD.

God is calling you, right where you are at, to choose today whom you will serve. I urge you to choose God and all He has for you. You will never regret it, because God's fingerprints of faithfulness will be all over your life for others to see! Someday, someone is going to look back on you and say, "I'm so glad she started right where she was. Her choice changed the course of my life."

Let's walk forward into this week deciding to either create or continue a godly legacy in our family. By yourself or with your family, pray about what kind of legacy you want to begin or continue. Don't be discouraged if you don't know where to start. Start with Jesus! Ask Him to help you. Look to others you trust and begin to make choices that reflect the image of God and His love for others.

Pray

Dear Lord, thank You that You are a God who cares about the legacy I leave over a lifetime. Even more, You care about eternal legacy in heaven. Today I commit to either starting or continuing a legacy that honors You. Thank You for the people who start godly legacies: parents, grandparents, mentors, and others. Give me the wisdom, creativity, and inspiration to be a faithful builder. Lord, help me to keep eternity in mind for everything I do. In Jesus' name, amen.

When we truly delight in the Lord, we also delight in the purposes and plans He has for us.

39

Delight in the Lord

Oh, the joys of those who do not follow the advice of the wicked, or stand around with sinners, or join in with mockers. But they delight in the law of the LORD, meditating on it day and night. They are like trees planted along the riverbank, bearing fruit each season. Their leaves never wither, and they prosper in all they do.

PSALM 1:1–3

GOD CALLS US TO DELIGHT IN HIM. And God created us with delight in His heart! We have always been His greatest creation. Even when you meet people who are far from the Lord, don't be fooled. Each and every one of us was created with purpose and delight in the heart of our good Father. It's through people's rejections and sin that they turn away from their Creator. Despite that, God still delights in those He loves. Psalm 147:11 tells us, "The LORD's delight is in those who fear him, those who put their hope in his unfailing love." That's us! Well, it can be us if we choose to put our hope in the Lord. And the benefit of delighting in the One who created us is a life of peace.

In Psalm 35:27, David writes, "Give great joy to those who came to my defense. Let them continually say, 'Great is the LORD, who delights in blessing his servant with peace!'" Peace is one of the greatest gifts God gives us. Not just the type that allows you to relax with no worries but God's peace. This is how Paul describes it in Philippians 4:7: "Then you will experience God's peace, which exceeds anything we can understand. His peace will guard your hearts and minds as you live in Christ Jesus." So not only does God delight in us, but when we regularly turn to Him in prayer and delight in Him, it comes back to us as peace that guards our hearts and minds.

When people picture God, they often think of a long list of rules and regulations. God does set boundaries in our lives. But picturing God this way misses an important piece of the puzzle. The reason God has set boundaries in our lives is so that we find true freedom in Him and delight in His ways.

How do we delight in the Lord? Here are a few practical ideas: read and meditate on God's Word; pray for yourself and others; call God your friend; enjoy His creation; recognize and thank Him for all the gifts He gives.

If you're married, think of how you delight in your husband. You communicate your love not only through your words but through your actions too. You may choose to create a specific atmosphere at home so that it is a place of rest for him. You may cook meals he enjoys to let him know you love him. You could even arrange for both of you to do his favorite activity to show that quality time matters! Over and over in your years of marriage, you will learn what brings your husband joy, and you can choose to do those things for him. All of these examples show how you delight in your husband and love him.

What about a friend? You may write a card telling them how much you appreciate them, or maybe you stop by to give them an encouraging hug. Our delight in God should be even greater than our delight in those we love on earth. He is our God, our Father, our Savior, our Advocate, our Friend, and so much more.

Although there are many benefits to delighting in the Lord, the Bible speaks about one very specifically in Psalm 37:4. "Take delight in the LORD, and he will give you your heart's desires." Wow! That's pretty exciting. But before we get too carried away thinking of all the things God could give us, it's important to understand something. We may think we know what we want. But when we truly delight in the Lord, we will find that our desires begin to shift. The things we once thought we wanted and needed may no longer be a priority. Why is that? Because when we truly delight in the Lord, we also delight in the purposes and plans He has for us. God's desires become our desires as our hearts align with His. And His ways are always, always more fulfilling and inspired than anything we could have thought up on our own. So when the Bible says that He will give us our heart's desires? It means God gives us what He's already purposed for our lives, which is the best gift we could ask for. All because we delighted in our Creator! Isn't that so cool?

Let's walk forward into this week choosing to purposefully delight in the Lord. Thank Him for His creation or how He has changed your life. Dig deep into relationship with Him by reading the Bible more consistently. Pray to Him with thanks and praise. However you can, as often as you can, delight in the Lord with all your heart!

Pray

Dear Lord, thank You that because You delighted in me and created me in Your image, I can live a life delighting in You. I'm humbled by Your goodness in my life. Your creation and its beauty bring me pleasure every day. I praise You that I am fearfully and wonderfully made and that You have purposes and plans for my life. I want to honor You in everything I say and do. Align my heart with Yours so that the desires of my heart match what You already have planned out for me. Thank You for caring about the details of my life in a way that I wouldn't even think of. God, Your ways are so much better than mine, and I want to bring You glory and make an impact for eternity. I freely choose to follow all that You have laid out for me, knowing that when I do, I'm walking in step with Your will for my life. I love You, Lord! I choose You over anything else and delight in who You are to me. In Jesus' name, amen.

We all have a story to tell, but that doesn't mean it's always our turn to tell it.

40

Words of Life

The tongue can bring death or life;
those who love to talk will reap the consequences.

PROVERBS 18:21

I'LL NEVER GET OVER the power of our words. How incredible is it that there's something we could say today that could stick with someone else for a lifetime? Everything we say matters—the way we talk about hard things, the way we talk to others, the way we talk to ourselves, the way we talk to and about our kids. What we say about ourselves is what spurs us to act, for better or for worse. So it makes sense that what we believe and say about others has the same effect on them. For better or for worse.

Whether you like it or not, our tongue is a weapon. The Bible says very plainly in James 3:6, "Among all the parts of the body, the tongue is a flame of fire. It is a whole world of wickedness, corrupting your entire body. It can set your whole life on fire, for it is set on fire by hell itself." If our tongue is naturally bent toward being corrupt, we have to be supernaturally transformed to use it in a way that glorifies the Lord and honors others. In other words, we need help with our words!

I have too many stories where I could not so proudly tell you, "Well, just the other day . . ." followed by how I wish I could take back what I said. But I'm on a mission to change that with the Lord's help. I recognize that the moments I don't use my words well usually stem from something deeper in my heart or come when I'm in some sort of spiritual drought. This kind of drought results from several factors, such as not listening to God in prayer and/or not being in

God's Word as much as I need to be. Another factor could be listening to the wrong voices and allowing those to influence how we use our words. Whatever it may be, we need to ask the Lord to help us find the root problem, ask for forgiveness, and ask Him to help us do better.

You aren't going to get better at anything just by taking all the right steps and checking all the boxes. We need to practice doing what is right so it becomes habit. From habit, it becomes a part of who we are. Our tongue is a muscle, and that muscle needs to be exercised in a healthy way. One of my kids' favorite stories is about the word *please*. The story depicts the word *please* as a little creature who lives inside your mouth. The more you use him, the more air he gets, which brings him life, health, and strength. The less you use him, the weaker he gets, and he doesn't have the energy to do what he is called to do. Our tongue needs to learn to speak life and words that build up others. The more we do this, the stronger our words of life will become. Pray out loud, practice right responses, and practice putting others first in conversation and being attentive to what they say. Even practice when *not* to speak.

According to James 3:10, blessing and cursing come out of the same mouth. Isn't it wild that just one thing—what we say—can make or break us? James 3:13 says, "If you are wise and understand God's ways, prove it by living an honorable life, doing good works with the humility that comes from wisdom." I love that biblical challenge and think we should all take it to heart. If you are wise . . . prove it! Show yourself and others that you can live a life that reflects what God has done in yours. But don't do it only for yourself. Do it for the glory of our Creator. The One who spoke the world into existence with words then gave us the gift of using our words to honor Him every day!

I also want to honor others, and one of the ways I can do that is by being attentive and showing value to who they are. Have you ever been talking to someone and you can almost see it in their eyes that instead of paying attention to what you are saying, they are just planning their response? That's frustrating, isn't it? I'm guilty of doing that! We've become such a me-first culture that we have forgotten that the true gospel calls us to be God-first and others-first.

We all have a story to tell, but that doesn't mean it's always our turn to tell it. When we begin to think that, we lose sight of the value of others in our lives. There is a time and place for your story, and God will give you the opportunity to share where He can be glorified the most. But when we try to consistently insert ourselves into every conversation, we only hurt and isolate ourselves and don't represent Jesus the way we should. As gracious people, we need to let others have time to share their stories. As attentive people, we need to show genuine interest in others so we have a right response. Not a preplanned, dismissive, or distracted response. But a right one that is "seasoned with salt" (Colossians 4:6, NIV). Because we care for others! We all know how much better food tastes with just the right amount of seasoning and salt. When we season our words and conversation like we season our food with salt, we may just discover things about other people we didn't know before. What an exciting opportunity to use our words well!

Let's walk forward into this week with a fresh plan on how we use our words. While in conversation, let's think about how what we say will affect others and reflect God. While at home, let's strengthen our habit of using words well, whether we are practicing kind responses or responding to our husband, children, roommates, or guests. What we say starts in our hearts and continues for our whole lives. This week, let's start (or restart) in the area of our words and aim for heaven in all we say!

Pray

Dear Lord, thank You for the gift of our words. I recognize that what I say carries power, and I want to speak in a way that is powerful for Your Kingdom. Lord, show me ways I can practice using my words well. Help me to start at home, creating a habit of choosing life-giving words. Help me to speak life over my spouse and my children and those within my immediate circle of relationships. In conversation, I want to prefer others. I want my words to be seasoned with salt so when others hear them, they get a taste of Your goodness and are drawn to You! Thank You for forgiving me when I've used my words to get my own way and tear others down. I want Your voice to be the loudest in my life, and I'm excited to use my words well for Your glory. In Jesus' name, amen.

God not
only sees the
bigger picture.
He *creates* the
bigger picture.

41

Would've, Should've, Could've

We can make our plans,
but the LORD determines our steps.

PROVERBS 16:9

DO YOU EVER WONDER how your life would've looked had you made different decisions? It's kind of crazy to think about, and I don't believe we can fully grasp the concept of how much life changes with each decision. Had any of us made even one or two different decisions—big or small—it could have changed everything that followed. Which is why it's so important to lean on the Lord for every decision we make and trust where He leads us. God has purposed and planned our lives to bring Him glory, which means He not only sees the bigger picture. He *creates* the bigger picture. And everything we set out to do should glorify Him.

Psalm 139:16 shows us how God ordains every season of our lives: "You saw me before I was born. Every day of my life was recorded in your book. Every moment was laid out before a single day had passed." When I look back on my time at college, I can see God's hand on my life at a time that was not my favorite. Freshman year, I had a few roommates, two of whom were teammates. We got along fine that year but weren't close. Year two, we were still friends and teammates, but it was more of the same story. I invited one of them to church every week, but she never came. When I left college after that year, I stayed in touch with that roommate. We became closer as we chatted on the phone often. Between her junior and senior year, she flew across the country, moved into my parents' house with me, and took an internship nearby. That summer, she rededicated her life to the Lord and began to live for Jesus. After graduating, she ended up moving into my parents' house and taking a full-time job. Over the years, she became like a bonus sister to me and bonus daughter in our family.

Years later, both her parents unexpectedly died far too soon. God knew long before any of us did that she would need a bonus family to walk through the rest of her life with. And He picked us. God chose a roommate that I had a minimal friendship with at a college that I really wasn't thrilled to be going to, and He turned it into something for His glory. To top off the story, she ended up marrying Tim's close childhood friend. Now they are both our best friends. It was a connection only God could make, and He did! It's not coincidence. It's our God. It's Psalm 139:16. It's how He loves us!

Do you have a story like that? One that has God's fingerprints all over it, and you can't deny how He made everything work together in an amazing way? Thank God again today for His goodness in your life. Tell Him how even though you tried to take things into your own hands, He used them for His glory. Or maybe you don't feel like that and you don't see God working in your life. Maybe you look at others who don't even follow the Lord and it seems they have it better than you. If that's the case, I want to encourage you with another verse. Proverbs 16:4 says, "The Lord has made everything for his own purposes, even the wicked for a day of disaster." What is this proverb telling us? It's confirming to us that the Lord is not weak and does not depend on people for success. God is in full control and makes no mistakes. Even those who choose to defy God—He still uses that to accomplish His will whether they follow Him or not. Without God, our plans will end in disaster.

I was asked one time, knowing what I know now about my less-than-desirable college athletics experience, would I do it all over again?

Instead of focusing on the disappointments of those years, I said, "How could I not? Did I love it? No. Was it miserable at times? Yes. But those two years brought one of the biggest blessings of our lives: a best friend and sister who became adopted into our family, adopted into God's family, and now is as much family as any of us." In other words, I wouldn't change a thing.

There is so much richness in God's ways and choosing His path. There is so much to gain when we ask for the Lord's wisdom in every decision we make and then trust Him to do the rest. We may think we are making all our own plans, but when we surrender those plans to the Lord, He will protect us and plot our every step so it brings glory to Him! That's the goal.

Let's walk forward into this week choosing to take every decision we make and give it to the Lord, asking for His wisdom. Let's also choose to trust in what He calls us to and where He calls us to go, knowing that He has every moment of our lives already laid out. If we recognize that we have been living with a "would've, should've, could've" attitude, let's quickly ask the Lord to help shift that mentality to one of knowing His purposes are better than we could have planned ourselves.

Pray

Dear Lord, thank You for fighting for me my whole life. And thank You even more that for every decision I make for myself, it's You who determines my steps. It's You who has plans and purposes for me that are yet to be revealed. Lord, I don't want to live a life of "would've, should've, could've." I want to live a life that is confident in You and confident in Your plans. I want Your plans to be my plans. I want Your thoughts to be my thoughts. And I want to fully trust in You, knowing that You've already written my story. Thank You for putting together all the pieces of my life to make way for what You've called me to do. This week and every week, I aim to walk in what You have for me. In Jesus' name, amen.

We won't
ever love
others like
God wants
us to if we
can't love
Him first.

42

Hard to Love

If you love only those who love you, why should you get credit for that? Even sinners love those who love them! And if you do good only to those who do good to you, why should you get credit? Even sinners do that much! . . . Love your enemies! Do good to them.

LUKE 6:32–33, 35

YOU KNOW THE PEOPLE. The ones who are *really* hard to love. The ones who share none of our interests or opinions. Sometimes it feels like pulling teeth just to find common ground. But the reality is we can also be those difficult people to someone else. Whenever I let my guard down and complain about someone I find difficult, Tim is quick to remind me, "And there are difficult things about us as well." Oof! Not what I wanted to hear, but the truth is all of us can be difficult people.

I was visiting with a good friend recently who owns her own business, and I asked how their company appreciation night went. She told me it was wonderful other than the fact that she really struggled to connect with a couple of employees whom she truly felt she had nothing in common with. And can I just say that this is my friend who probably wins the award for valuing and loving others so intentionally and well! So if she is struggling, imagine how the rest of us are doing. She said she tried so hard to find some point of common ground only to come up short.

But it's what she said at the end of our talk that I valued most. "I just always want people to feel valued and loved and seen no matter whether they are like me or not. So I'm going to push through and find a way to do that."

Wow! I know that about her, but when she said it, I could hear her heart. And that's the type of heart I want to have for others when I find them hard to love. Why? Because that's how I want people to love me even when I'm difficult and hard to love.

No matter who we are, all of us have an instinctual need to feel loved. But we must also love others. How do we do that, especially when we don't feel like it? In the Bible, a religious leader attempted to stump Jesus by asking Him what the greatest commandment was. In Mark 12:29-31, "Jesus replied, 'The most important commandment is this: "Listen, O Israel! The Lord our God is the one and only Lord. And you must love the Lord your God with all your heart, all your soul, all your mind, and all your strength." The second is equally important: "Love your neighbor as yourself." No other commandment is greater than these.'" You know as well as I do that there are a lot of important commandments from God. If Jesus elevates this one, we better pay attention.

I love that Jesus starts with loving the Lord. We can do a lot of things in our own strength—for a little while at least. But trying to do it all on our own will wear us out quick. We weren't created to do things alone. We were created for community and for others. But most of all, we were created for the Lord and for His delight. Our first aim should be to love the Lord with all our heart, mind, and strength just as the Bible instructs us. This builds the foundation for being able to love others. We won't ever love others like God wants us to if we can't love Him first.

Our culture would tell you that you can love however you want—and, most of all, love yourself first. Please don't believe that lie today or any other day. Notice in the Bible that we are *never* commanded to put ourselves first at the expense of others. In fact, 2 Timothy 3:2-3 tells us that, in the end times, people will only love themselves and will be unloving and unforgiving. Lord, keep me far from that attitude. Let's choose to set our sights on God. When we love Him, we love ourselves by default because He created us in His image. We can be confident of this when we are confident of our identity in Christ. If we aren't, let's get there first. How? By asking the Lord who He made us to be and calls us to be! It's truly all full circle, but it starts with loving God.

The second commandment comes after the first because, again, we can't love others well when we aren't loving the Lord well and knowing who we are called to be. You've probably heard the saying that it's hard to pour out of an empty cup. That's true. But with Jesus in our hearts and at the center of our lives, we can love others out of the overflow of our own life. We will be able to show and express a kind of love that doesn't fade with our emotions. The heart of God is for everyone, and as people made in God's image, we should be for everyone too. Yes, even if they don't act/look/eat/live/talk/exercise just like us. Since we all have our own unique giftings of how we interact with people, we will be able to interact with some people whom others struggle with (and vice versa). But that shouldn't stop us from stretching ourselves to show kindness, encouragement, or love.

It's easy to look for ways to get ahead at the expense of others. But when we choose to love people, we view life as a journey rather than a competition. This attitude exchanges comfort for discomfort when necessary. I admire Tim because he is so good at prioritizing the needs of others at his workplace. He manages around ninety employees with a variety of personalities. Yet what I notice about Tim is he always finds a way to make others feel valued. When we put Mark 12:31 into practice in any area—whether work, family, or other relationships—we will be walking in obedience to God while also bringing joy to ourselves and those around us.

As we walk forward into this week, let's find someone within our sphere who we find hard to love. Choose to go to that person and have a simple conversation to learn more about them. You never know—maybe you will be surprised at what you learn. Either way, they will experience your love and the love of Jesus through how you valued them.

Pray

Dear Lord, I need Your help to love others well and to do it in a genuine way. I may not know their history with You, but I know *my* history with You, and I want to show others who You are. Lord, I want to be the type of person who loves other people, even when we don't see eye to eye or have much in common. Help me to not give up just because someone is difficult for me—after all, I know I can be difficult for others. Give me wisdom on how to be intentionally kind even when I don't feel like it. I want to value what You value, Lord. In Jesus' name, amen.

God takes our brokenness and specializes in making it beautiful.

43

Close to the Brokenhearted

Since we have a great High Priest who has entered heaven, Jesus the Son of God, let us hold firmly to what we believe. This High Priest of ours understands our weaknesses, for he faced all of the same testings we do, yet he did not sin. So let us come boldly to the throne of our gracious God. There we will receive his mercy, and we will find grace to help us when we need it most.

HEBREWS 4:14-16

I WAS JUST A YEAR AND A HALF OLD when my mom and dad lost my little brother in the womb. He was the fifth child and second boy in our family of one boy and three girls—a blessing they didn't expect but were thrilled to welcome. I remember staying at a house with friends of my parents for a couple nights. Then my siblings and I went home, and it was as if nothing had changed. Yet for my parents, everything had changed. At six months pregnant, my mom had given birth to my brother, who was no longer alive. It's hard for me to comprehend what a massive loss they went through. It took my mom years to come out of the fog of grief and see how God could possibly make beauty from ashes. Now it's been over three decades since she lost my little brother. Although the grief is still there, she has a new perspective that took years to gain. Here is what my mom shared with me:

> That loss sent me into probably the most awful point of my life. I honestly don't know how my children were mothered and taken care of, but they were. The sadness made it hard for me to keep going. But I had a couple friends who stood with me and walked me through it. My pastor's wife

would just come and sit on the floor of my bedroom as I lay in bed. These friends really saw me through that time. For about the first twenty-five years, whenever I talked about Daniel, I would cry. I still cry. But in more recent years, it's gotten less painful. We always told ourselves that Daniel was short-circuited to heaven and got to bypass life to be with Jesus. Something that was so hard for me but that comforted me.

The thing that helped me the most—and this is what I would say to women who have lost a child or have a friend who lost a child—is validating that my baby was real. He isn't here anymore, and I don't have any memories with him, but people remembering is so huge. People asking his name. Asking details about his birth. Asking what he looked like. It kept him real because he was real.

All I know is I was hurting so bad, and I just leaned into the Lord because I needed Him. Little by little, He has healed me. He's taken a lot of broken pieces and made them beautiful in my life. I honestly don't think I would be the person I am today if I hadn't walked through losing Daniel. I died to myself, and the Lord birthed new things in me. I was able to identify with Jesus' suffering a bit more, as the Bible says. Christ was formed new in me. Things that would've been just head knowledge are now emotional, and I can empathize with others. I wish I wasn't able to relate, but I am. And the areas the Lord uses me in today to love on others, get outside myself, and encourage others is only because of the work He's done in me over the years. I also had to learn to communicate in my marriage better and work toward healing in our lives.

What God also worked in me as a mother was to understand and treasure my children more. To be more empathetic and sympathetic with them even though that wasn't natural to me. To be able to recognize a hurting person a lot more easily than I would've before experiencing loss. Our default when we are hurting and feel like we are swallowed up in depression and grief is to wall off and be alone. But we can't do that. Don't give in to the tendency to isolate. We have to press the opposite way and make ourselves vulnerable and communicate because other people can't read your mind. It's okay to say, "I'm hurting today" and to fall apart in front of others and let them cover you in prayer and love. Every falling apart is a step closer to healing your heart.

And here's the other side of the story. My brother's name was Daniel Timothy. Prior to meeting my husband, the Lord had prompted me to "pray for a Daniel." When I met my husband, I soon found out that not only was his name, Timothy Daniel, the reverse of my brother's, but that they were the same age by a few months. When my mom met Tim, she said she knew right away that we would be married. Later on, she told me why: "Right when I met him and saw his bright smile and blondish hair, the Lord spoke to my spirit, *This is going to be your son I'm giving back to you after all these years.* God, in all His goodness and foreknowledge, had been preparing this moment that would heal my heart."

Whether you are currently walking through a loss or have walked through one in the past, know today that God takes our brokenness and specializes in making it beautiful. You may not see it today, tomorrow, or for three decades—you may not even see it this side of heaven. But it doesn't mean He isn't working behind the scenes for our good and His glory. The Bible tells us in Psalm 34:18, "The Lord is close to the brokenhearted; he rescues those whose spirits are crushed." The beautiful thing about our God is that He is exactly what you need in whatever season you are facing. We just need to remember what my mom said: "Every falling apart is a step closer to healing your heart."

Let's walk forward into this week with a sensitive heart. If someone you know is facing a loss in their life, choose to be the friend who shows up and walks with them. The one who sits next to them in silence just so they aren't alone.

And when the timing is right, ask them about the loss and remember the person who was dear to them. If you are facing loss, be vulnerable and communicate so others can help be a part of your healing. These are both hard things to do, but they're worth doing!

Pray

Dear Lord, thank You that You are near to the brokenhearted. I will never know all the whys behind everything I experience in life, but what I do know is that it is all part of the story you have written for me. Lord, would You take the pieces of my heart that have been shattered and heal them? Would You turn my pain into a testimony of Your faithfulness? And most of all, please never let me walk through loss alone. Place people around me who will hold up my arms when I can't do it anymore. Who will speak words of life into the parts of me that feel dead. Thank You, Lord, that as I look back over my life, I can see Your fingerprints on every situation. I trust You in the good and I trust You in the hard. In Jesus' name, amen.

We can begin habits today that will make a difference in our relationship with the Lord forever.

44

Healthy Habits

My dear brothers and sisters, be strong and immovable. Always work enthusiastically for the Lord, for you know that nothing you do for the Lord is ever useless.

1 CORINTHIANS 15:58

MY KIDS WERE ASKING ME a while back what it was like when I worked as a registered nurse at a hospital. Questions like: What area did I work in? Did I ever deliver babies? Do I know as much as doctors? Can I help deliver babies? Was I good at nursing school? Would I be able to deliver my own babies since I'm a nurse? I love kids and how they think, and clearly mine had a theme going with their questions—they love babies!

As I was answering their questions, sharing what it was like to be a nurse and what kinds of patients I took care of, the thing that stuck out to me the most was the repetition. I worked on a unit where a lot of the same surgeries happened week in and week out, so we took care of many patients who needed to accomplish the same steps before being released home. A lot of nursing is this way: morning rounds, assessments, medications, check-ins, answering call lights, bathing, toileting, feeding, then back to assessing again. For the type of nursing I did, shifts didn't vary too much from this routine. Sure, each day was a little different, but consistency was key.

Christianity requires the same type of consistency and attention to detail nurses provide. Following Jesus is exciting and life-changing and filled with unexpected God moments. But following Jesus also requires us to be consistent so when the awesome mountaintop moments fade back to normal, we aren't left wondering what happened. And when the really tough valley experiences linger longer than we'd like, we need a foundation to stand on.

How do we build a consistent habit? Just like anything else, start one day, do it again the next and the next, and keep on going. Slowly we train ourselves in a new habit. And just like with any habit, we have to start somewhere and keep going. If we let up a day, we don't mope around and give up. We simply start where we left off, knowing that we have the capability to train ourselves in anything we set our minds to. We can begin habits today that will make a difference in our relationship with the Lord forever. And when we get out of step or miss a day, we can just start again.

When we mess up or miss the mark on a spiritual discipline, sometimes we don't want to start again. We feel a myriad of emotions ranging from shame and guilt to despair and frustration. That is exactly the tactic the enemy likes to use. If he can convince us of our failure, he wins. So know that those negative feelings and thoughts aren't from the Lord. Because God is not a god of shame and despair. He is a God who forgives and overcomes, and He doesn't want us to stay stuck where we are. He wants us to overcome with His help.

One way we can establish good habits is by surrounding ourselves with good company who models by example. Proverbs 13:20 says, "Walk with the wise and become wise; associate with fools and get in trouble." We need God's wisdom and guidance from wise mentors to help us establish healthy habits that will bear fruit in our lives. When I look at the people in my life who exemplify a healthy walk with the Lord, I see two habits right away: reading their Bible daily and praying daily. We need to treat reading our Bible as if it's necessary for survival in our daily lives. Having God's Word in our hearts and knowing Him more fully allows us to tap into His strength and wisdom whenever we need it. We can also do that by praying daily. This doesn't have to be a long, drawn-out process (although there may be times we spend many hours on our knees in prayer, petitioning the Lord). We can pray anytime throughout our day. We can pray as we make a meal, fold laundry, bathe our kids, take a walk, and spend our quiet time in the Word. I call my parents and friends all the time to just check in and chat about life. How much more do we need to be doing this with the Lord? We are His delight, and He is ours. So let's invite Him into our lives.

Establishing habits to connect with the Lord will yield similar but even better results since they are eternal. We can show up every day ready to serve Him. We can read our Bible and pray even when we don't feel like it, knowing that our feelings don't dictate our habits or our consistency. We can intentionally choose a right attitude even when we have every reason to choose a wrong one. And the fruit that these basic habits will bear literally builds a foundation of trust in the Lord.

I sang a classic children's song when I was a kid, and I still sing it to my boys. "Read your Bible, pray every day and you'll grow, grow, grow" followed by "Forget your Bible, forget to pray and you'll shrink, shrink, shrink." This is all the motivation we need to establish consistent habits for our walk with Christ. Building ourselves up and establishing consistent practices in our lives is building a solid foundation so when the waters get rough and the world tosses us around, we can rely on God's truth hidden in our hearts. We can build Jesus a home in our hearts that is built on God's truth and relies solely on Him through every season and circumstance.

Let's walk forward into this week starting (or restarting) a habit of reading our Bible and praying every day. Make it doable for yourself each day by maybe reading one chapter in your Bible (start with the book of Matthew or James) and saying one short prayer after you read. Aim to do this for one week. Once you accomplish that, aim for the next. Before you know it, a habit will form, and the Lord will become the most important part of your everyday life. From there, it will just keep getting better!

Dear Lord, I want to know You more and grow in my relationship with You all the days of my life. Sometimes that feels hard to keep up with. I do well for a while, but then I miss a day and feel thrown off. But I don't want to let the enemy have a voice in my head just because I've missed the mark. I want to form good habits that focus on You, and I can't do that in my own strength. Will You help me establish consistency to do the things You've called me to do? Whether that's reading the Bible, praying, or asking You to carry my burdens and handle the circumstances of my life. Lord, teach me how to know You more through Your Word and through prayer. I pray that I would hear Your voice each and every day as I invite You into all I do. In Jesus' name, amen.

Once you
know the
goodness
of God
and taste
His grace
and mercy
in your life,
you won't
want to
go back.

45

Choose True Joy

Bless the LORD, O my soul,
and forget not all his benefits,
who forgives all your iniquity,
who heals all your diseases,
who redeems your life from the pit,
who crowns you with steadfast love and mercy.

PSALM 103:2-4, ESV

LET'S CONTRAST TWO VERSES that show two very different attitudes we can have in life. Then we can decide which one we want to follow.

> Dear brothers and sisters, one final thing. Fix your thoughts on what is true, and honorable, and right, and pure, and lovely, and admirable. Think about things that are excellent and worthy of praise.
>
> PHILIPPIANS 4:8

> For people will love only themselves and their money. They will be boastful and proud, scoffing at God, disobedient to their parents, and ungrateful. They will consider nothing sacred. They will be unloving and unforgiving; they will slander others and have no self-control. They will be cruel and hate what is good.
>
> 2 TIMOTHY 3:2-3

If you had to choose which type of person you want to be, I'm assuming you would overwhelmingly choose the first. Even if you don't believe in Jesus, it's hard to deny that the first mindset is a far better choice for how to live. If that's the case, why don't we always live according to the first? Because of sin. Sin has made it hard to choose the better way—the way God intended for us to live. With all the distractions of life, it can feel hard sometimes to choose what is true and right and honorable when it's not as fun or fulfilling in our eyes. But when we are followers of Jesus, it's not just about us—what we want or what we think will bring us pleasure. It's about obeying God's eternal Word, which brings a whole host of gifts and benefits. So it comes down to a choice between temporary pleasure and eternal joy. And we get to choose.

Once we make that choice, we have to start lining up every area of our lives with the Word of God. Can I just tell you that this is the really hard part? The decision to follow God feels big, but after that, starting to obey Him in every other area of life is just as important. This usually doesn't feel good in the beginning, but it will be worth all the sacrifice. The good news is God has given us the gift of the Holy Spirit to help us with every area and decision in our life. Once we give our lives to Jesus, we stop living for earthly pleasures. The other good news is, when we give up what seems important or exciting, we see that it's nothing compared to what we gain: "love, joy, peace, patience, kindness, goodness, faithfulness, gentleness, and self-control" (Galatians 5:22-23). And that's just a start. We gain the Holy Spirit as our everyday Advocate and Counselor. We gain direct access to heaven and a relationship with our heavenly Father. Whether you grew up with a wonderful dad or one who wasn't present at all, my guess is you know the value of having a good father. And God is that for all of us. Most of all, we gain freedom in Christ to live out His purposes for our life—purposes that are far better than anything we could dream up for ourselves.

How do we get there? We use Philippians 4:8 as our guide and standard for how God wants us to live. Since this verse tells us to "fix [our] thoughts" on certain things, we know that we can use those standards to guide our decision-making. For example, we can ask ourselves questions like these: *Are the conversations I take part in true? Are the shows I watch honorable? Are the ways I choose to live right and pure? Are the words I speak about others lovely? Are the ways I do my work admirable?*

Chances are that, as we start asking those questions from Philippians, we probably will answer "no" to at least one. Then we have another choice. Do we keep watching the shows or listening to the music that isn't honorable? Do we keep choosing to live in sin or impurity knowing that what we are doing isn't acceptable to the Lord? Do we keep speaking words that aren't lovely and taking actions that aren't admirable?

Once you know the goodness of God and taste His grace and mercy in your life, you won't want to go back. Leaving behind what you know feels painful, but rejecting His commands to live the holy life He's called us to would be even more painful. Before you knew Jesus, sin may have seemed to bring you joy. But the true joy God has for us when we live according to His ways is so much better.

In order to access that joy, we can hold up everything that influences us to our biblical measuring standard: true, honorable, right, pure, lovely, admirable. And if it doesn't make the cut, I pray we have the strength to choose what's of the Lord and not what's of this world. And that when we do, we see the blessing that follows as we take each step into deeper relationship with the Lord.

Let's walk forward into this week asking God to give us wisdom for the areas of our lives that need an overhaul. Let's ask Him to give us keen eyes to discern what we should let in and what we should keep out based on our biblical measuring stick. When He reveals those areas, let's obey those promptings from the Holy Spirit.

Pray

Dear Lord, thank You so much for giving me the ability to know You and choose Your ways over the ways of the world. I want to live rightly before You because I know there is freedom in living for Your Kingdom. I also know it isn't guaranteed to be easy, but You will give me wisdom in every situation. Lord, help me to take everything that passes before me and line it up with Your Word. I want to make choices that are true, honorable, right, pure, lovely, and admirable. I want to choose these things because I want to choose You each and every day. I know it won't be easy, and it will probably mean making sacrifices. But give me the strength to make those choices, and help me to see that Your joy is greater than anything I've experienced before. I trust that what You have for me is better than I can imagine. In Jesus' name, amen.

We can do uncomfortable things if the Lord is calling us to them.

46

Step Out in Faith

The disciples went everywhere and preached, and the Lord worked through them, confirming what they said by many miraculous signs.

MARK 16:20

MY MOM OFTEN TELLS ME, "There are things I don't want to do that aren't my natural gifting, but I do them because they're right or God calls me to do them. And usually these are the areas that have the most impact, even though I feel like they're the areas I'm least qualified in." I appreciate those honest words—they're a reminder that I often need to hear. Sometimes in life, it's easy to get stuck doing what we are good at. I know I do it. I am comfortable in what I know, and to be stretched outside of that is an inconvenience and takes effort. Effort that I might not have the capacity or desire for. I'd rather run on autopilot than have to plot a new course.

We can also get into autopilot mode when it comes to Christianity and serving the Lord. Go to church, worship God, read your Bible, serve in an area that interests you, be generous, love others, and repeat every Sunday until we die. Do you ever feel that way? Like you are just going through the cycle over and over, and nothing ever really changes, but hey, at least you are doing the right things, right? This type of attitude is the opposite of what God calls us to.

I always love seeing someone come to know Jesus for the first time. If you've ever talked to someone who recently gave their life to the Lord, you can hardly wipe the smile off their face. They are willing to do *anything* for the Kingdom of God, and they can't contain His goodness inside. It doesn't matter if they know how to share the Good News or not, they just want a chance to be a part of spreading God's Kingdom. The reality is that as Christians, even "seasoned" ones, we should be inspiring. None of us should ever lose that zeal for God's purposes and what He calls us to and equips us for. When we do, people might see two very different sides of Christianity: one that's bland and boring and the other that's exuberant and exciting. We should all want the second description for our lives because the goal is to lead people to Jesus, not turn them off to Him.

As I mentioned before, it's easy to get into a cycle of mindless, routine Christianity. But if that's the case, we're being Christian robots—and, therefore, we need a reboot! Being a follower of Jesus calls us to a life of excitement and takes us to known and unknown places where we learn about real relationship with Christ and how to live for eternity. Does that mean every moment will be exciting? No, we may not always feel excitement like that. But it does mean we have lasting joy in Jesus as a foundation. And along the way in this journey, we also learn about who we are called to be and what we are called to do in God's Kingdom. Yes, certain seasons may be hard or mundane, but we've got the King of the universe on our side. We already know who wins and how the story ends, so our excitement should be pretty contagious. How do we keep it that way? By living out what we are purposed to do and being willing to step outside of our natural giftings.

It's generally easier and more comfortable to do something we already know how to do. For most of our parenting years, Tim and I have chosen to serve in the kids' ministry at our church. Why? Because we've had babies and toddlers for so long—it's easy to serve in nursery or pre-K classes since our children are already there. Holding and rocking babies, reading books, playing with toys, and teaching lessons on loving Jesus and others definitely comes naturally to us right now.

But what happens when we are called to serve in an area that we don't have a natural desire for or gifting in? Do we just say, "Oh that's not something I'm good at, so I'll pass," even though there is a need? Maybe. Or maybe we view it as an opportunity to grow and allow the Lord to develop something new inside us, all while filling a need!

If I'm comfortable in kids' church but someone asks me to be on a prayer team, what if that's the Lord calling and stretching me to deepen my prayer life with Him? Maybe I'm not naturally gifted as a teacher, but the Lord is calling me to homeschool my kids for a season. Maybe I'm not that great at hosting, but the Holy Spirit prompts me to open up my home to a group of people each week. We can do uncomfortable things if the Lord is calling us to them. We can be open to what the Lord calls each of us to do rather than dismissing anything outside our comfort zone.

My mom has been running a "grandmas group" for several years now. She's naturally gifted at encouraging but has had to grow in the area of speaking out loud to a group. Yet this once-a-month gathering of grandmas has impacted so many. My mom's yes allowed the Lord to work through her to accomplish His will for others to grow in their relationship with Him. It's so amazing to me that the Lord can use us in any area, whether we are gifted or not, to advance His purposes and His Kingdom. We just have to be willing to hear His voice and say yes when He calls. We can't let pride get in the way. Everything we do should be for the Lord and His Kingdom even if it's outside of our normal routines.

Let's walk forward into this week asking the Holy Spirit to increase our capacity to do what God has called us to even if it's outside what we feel capable of. Also, ask the Holy Spirit to grow you in supernatural ways as you step into areas that might feel unknown or scary. Remember that God completely knows you and will never lead you down a wrong path.

Pray

Dear Lord, thank You for all the opportunities You give me to serve You and have an impact for the Kingdom of God. I know that You have uniquely gifted me in certain areas of life. But I also want to be open to areas that don't come as naturally to me. I know that trying new things and taking new opportunities will help me grow, and I don't want to miss an opportunity that You put before me. Help me choose to obey and follow through on what You have commanded. Give me wisdom for what You want me to say yes to, and equip me to do those things with all my heart. Thank You that You are a God who sees the bigger picture. Help me to see the bigger picture as well. In Jesus' name, amen.

We cannot expect to have a healthy marriage when all we do is play defense.

47

Play Offense

From the beginning, "God made them male and female." . . . "This explains why a man leaves his father and mother and is joined to his wife, and the two are united into one." Since they are no longer two but one, let no one split apart what God has joined together.

MATTHEW 19:4–6

WHAT A GIFT a godly marriage is—which explains why marriage is so heavily under attack. The devil hates marriage and everything it stands for. He hates unity and loves destruction. He hates multiplication and loves division. So any way he can destroy marriage, he will. Whether through distractions or distortions, the enemy is looking for a way to get in. And when we enter the marriage covenant, we must be on our guard to protect what God has given us.

I grew up playing sports, and I can tell you they all had one thing in common. You won more points playing offense than you did defense. There were times when a team would be so strong and so overwhelming that all you could do was defend. But once you got on offense again? You better take advantage and score those points to secure the win. Marriage is much the same. We cannot expect to have a healthy marriage when all we do is play defense. Offense builds, protects, and secures against the enemy.

Prayer is one of the biggest things we can do to go on the offense. Through prayer, God literally changes lives. When we try to do it ourselves, it usually doesn't end the way we hope. I remember there was something in our marriage that I felt so strongly about and wanted Tim to also feel strongly about. But he didn't. After a few months of trying to will it into him on my own, I realized I had been going about it all the wrong way. The Lord is in charge of Tim's heart.

Not me. And we have to remember that our spouses aren't the only ones who have areas needing change and improvement.

So I started praying. Notice how I didn't say I started praying for Tim. Trust me, that's usually my default. *Lord, help Tim do better at this and this and this. Amen.* Let me encourage you to be careful with those types of prayers. What is our motivation? Is it for our husbands to become more like Jesus or more like us? When we pray for our husbands, our prayer should be that the Lord would work in their hearts to be more like Him. And then we should pray the same thing for ourselves. We can trust that the Lord will be faithful to do just that for both of us. Because He will in His way and His timing.

Months later, as I continued to pray for both Tim and myself, something really special happened. The thing I had been praying for began to slowly show up in Tim's life. This was also a healthy reminder to me that I shouldn't try to force him to change. The good news is we don't have to wait till something bad happens to pray for our husbands. We can pray for them all the time. Prayer is powerful and makes a difference in people's lives—and it makes a difference in our marriages. Amen!

Another area of marriage where we can play offense is in how we communicate and use our words. This is something Tim and I wish we had been better about from the beginning. It's an area we now work hard to be intentional at every day. It's gotten better with practice, but we know we can never let down our guard. The devil loves to use our words to get us into trouble. The first several years of our marriage, I assumed a whole lot. Like the fact that Tim would know exactly what I needed exactly when I needed it. I dug myself into a hole of discontentment while Tim wondered what in the world was going on with his wife. All of this could've been avoided with good communication. Words shouldn't be used or held against your spouse to get what you want. That will never end well. But words used in the right way? Proverbs 16:24 tells us, "Kind words are like honey—sweet to the soul and healthy for the body." Let's let our words reflect that in every situation.

Listening is a third way we can be proactive to build up our marriage. When we take the time to understand what someone else is saying, it builds unity. Without saying anything, we're communicating that we care and that we value who they are and what they have to say. It also sets an example for how we'd like to be treated.

Lastly, do things together. Remember that you got married so you could be together. The enemy hates that because he knows how powerful walking in unity is. When Tim and I got married, my cousin, who was our wedding coordinator and had been married a long time, gave me this advice: "When you are at your wedding reception, go greet people *together*." She told us it's so easy for newlyweds to say "I do," then walk into their reception and go to their friends separately to say hi and receive congratulations. But that was our first opportunity to do something together and show that we were united. Looking back, I know the value that advice carries. Doing things together sets a tone for your marriage and shows everyone—including your children if you become parents—that you are "team each other."

Let's walk forward into this week evaluating these four areas of our marriage: prayer, communication, listening, and togetherness. That's just a start, but it's a good start. Wherever you are in marriage—thriving or needing help, married many years or just starting out—you can commit to building up, protecting, and defending your marriage. Don't let the enemy use what has been to dictate what will be. Start where you are, and expect the Lord to do the miraculous in you and your marriage.

Pray

Dear Lord, marriage is a gift from You, and I pray that I would steward it well. Help me to look to You and put You first in everything. To ask for Your wisdom and let You into every area of my marriage. Would You soften my heart to hear Your voice and help me listen to the Holy Spirit for how to live rightly with my husband? Lord, I pray that my husband would be strong and lead well and that You would give me wisdom to support him. I pray that when we come to a tough season of marriage, that Your peace and counsel would come in to help us reset on the right course together. Lord, let the work that we are putting in now bring a season of thriving and of rest. Thank You that, no matter what I am facing, all it takes is *one day* for change to happen. You are the God of one day! In Jesus' name, amen.

Stay the course and keep your saltiness.

48

Team Jesus

You are the salt of the earth. But what good is salt if it has lost its flavor? Can you make it salty again? It will be thrown out and trampled underfoot as worthless. You are the light of the world—like a city on a hilltop that cannot be hidden. No one lights a lamp and then puts it under a basket. Instead, a lamp is placed on a stand, where it gives light to everyone in the house. In the same way, let your good deeds shine out for all to see, so that everyone will praise your heavenly Father.

MATTHEW 5:13-16

AS HUMANS, IF WE BELIEVE in something strongly enough, we will back up whatever it is to anyone willing to listen. In today's culture, we can just find the facts that line up with our beliefs and blast those without ever doing our due diligence. But no matter what this life throws at us, we can align ourselves with the ultimate truth—God's truth—every time. He defines what is right and what is wrong. No matter the subject, our eyes are called to stay focused on what's most important: the Kingdom of God. The Bible refers to Jesus followers as salt. Salt has played an important role in the lives of God's people since the earliest biblical times.

When the Israelites were wandering for forty years, the Lord gave them many rules and regulations to follow when it came to sacrifices for uncleanliness or atoning for sins. Leviticus 2:13 says every grain sacrifice that was made had to be seasoned with salt. Why? So these sacrifices would taste better to God? You wouldn't be too far off with that argument. Sacrifices were considered a pleasing aroma to God (see Leviticus 1:9 and 2:2). But salt was also a precious commodity. It was expensive and valuable. Adding salt to a sacrifice increased its value.

making the sacrifice even more precious. So when God calls us the "salt of the earth," He is placing value on us. We are precious to Him.

But what happens when we lose our saltiness? Do we become less precious to Him? No. But we do lose our effectiveness. When you salt your food, you want it to taste more flavorful. Likewise, God wants us to know and live by His truth every day so we can be effective in sharing Him with the world. If we aren't doing what we are called to do—preach the gospel of Jesus—then we lose our effectiveness. We lose our saltiness. And instead of people looking to Jesus for answers, they will start looking somewhere else.

We like to tell our kids that we are "Team Us." Sometimes Tim says he's on "Team Mom," and I might also say I am on "Team Dad." What we mean by this is that, no matter what, we work together as one. Sometimes our kids will ask Tim something, and if they don't like his answer, they will find me and ask the same question. In this situation, I would say, "Did you already ask your dad?" If the answer is yes, then I reply with "Okay. Well, I'm Team Dad, so whatever his answer was, that's my answer too." It's a really great way to show our kids that we are on the same team. Sure, we make mistakes, but we also have a game plan to be on the same page so our kids have a consistent voice in their lives. They know we care for them enough not to be wishy-washy with each other. If we don't back each other up, we will lose our effectiveness as parents, and they might go looking to other sources for answers.

The same goes for the Lord. He is the consistent voice in our lives. When the world says something confusing or misleading, we can read the Bible to access God's truth. People have varying opinions on highly debated topics, so we should ask God for His wisdom on how to speak truth and love into the conversation. It should be clear to people that, no matter what we are facing or what we are talking about, we are always "Team Jesus" and on the side of God's truth with our voice! And we need to do as Colossians 4:6 instructs: "Let your conversation be always full of grace, seasoned with salt, so that you may know how to answer everyone" (NIV). God is calling us, His precious and highly valued creation, to be a light to a dark world. God is also calling us not to lose our effectiveness for His Kingdom by getting lost in the ways of the world. We must dig deep into God's Word so we can hide the truth in our hearts to guard against stumbling away and sinning against God (see Psalm 119:11).

How can we be a light? By choosing not to hide. Sometimes I don't want to ruffle any feathers in hard conversations, so I end up not saying anything. But God didn't call us to be silent on every issue. And even when He does ask us to stay quiet, He still calls us to shine His light by our good deeds. When we do good deeds with the right heart, people see Jesus through us. The Lord can use our good deeds to draw people to praise His name. We need both: salt and light. There is no either-or. By being both salt and light, we tell and show others that we are "Team Jesus" all the way to heaven! Stay the course and keep your saltiness. God has given you everything you need to live rightly before the Lord and shine your light so others can do the same. Stick with the truth of God instead of the ever-changing message the world will try to convince you to believe. Theirs is a "truth" that wavers, but God's truth stands firm.

Let's walk forward into this week choosing to be on Team Jesus. When you have an opportunity to speak about Him, let your words be seasoned with salt. Choose to proclaim God's truth with grace in the middle of everything being said around you. Keep your saltiness by staying in God's Word. When you don't have anything to say, let your right actions and good deeds speak for themselves. You never know how He might work in the hearts of those who are listening.

Pray

Dear Lord, thank You that You give me everything I need to live for You. Sometimes I forget that, and I try to do things in my own strength. But I want to rely on You so I can be effective for Your Kingdom. In everything I say and do, I want others to wonder where my strength comes from so I can tell them about Your goodness and love. Lord, help me not only to speak with Your truth, love, and grace to others, but also help me model those attributes. Will You season my conversations and words with salt so they are a delight to You and to those I'm speaking to? I don't want to hide out, so help me be bold to preach the gospel to everyone around me. I love You, Lord, and I want others to experience Your love like I have. Help them to see You in me so Your name can be glorified. In Jesus' name, amen.

Anything we have worked hard to achieve is because God gave us the ability to do so.

49

In Christ Alone

I can do everything through Christ, who gives me strength.

PHILIPPIANS 4:13

SOMETIMES I WONDER if we really believe what we read in the Bible. For example: the Olympics took place recently, and over the course of several weeks, our family watched various sporting events and competitions. Typically, whenever someone won, the TV reporters were right there to interview them and get their initial reactions and thoughts. They asked questions like "How do you feel about winning? Did you think you could do it? What pushed you today to finish so strongly?" It was interesting to hear the athletes' answers. Some athletes did give glory to God and acknowledged the role that others played in their victory, while many other athletes relayed a sense of self-promotion and self-sufficiency.

As a former competitive athlete, I'm all for a sense of pride and accomplishment after a job well done. But the message I heard from an abundance of various athletes was one of "I did this! I worked hard and got to where I am." Which, of course, they did. But leaving it at that doesn't acknowledge where their talents and giftings came from or the fact that they didn't do it alone. It sounds more like "I can do all things in myself." According to a philosophy like this, we don't need anyone else's help. We just have to work hard, overcome, and push through—and we can win gold in sports and in life. This definitely made for some interesting conversations with our children about where our strength comes from and who we are living life for. Is it just for recognition and accomplishments, or is there something more to life than achieving our own dreams and goals?

Even our kids recognized that the sentiments expressed by most winners seemed very self-centered. We began to ask and answer questions like "Where does our strength come from?" and "Can we do all things ourselves?" Let's answer the first question through the lens of Christ and all He's done for us. Psalm 121:2 says, "My help comes from the LORD, who made heaven and earth." Because we believe in God's Word as truth, we can say with confidence that our strength comes from the Lord. The God who made heaven and earth also chose to create us. God created each of us to live out His will for our lives—and it's up to us to follow and glorify Him in all we do. Anything we have worked hard to achieve is because God gave us the ability to do so. Check out 1 Corinthians 8:6, which tells us, "There is one God, the Father, by whom all things were created, and for whom we live." However our body functions and however our mind is wired, both are gifts we should not take for granted. We need to daily thank God for the abilities He's uniquely given each of us and know that it was on purpose with a purpose.

To answer the second question, when we know God and choose to not acknowledge His place in our lives, claiming we're doing everything by our own strength, we stand in direct opposition to God's Word. Malachi 2:2 gives this warning: "'If you do not listen, and if you do not resolve to honor my name,' says the LORD Almighty, 'I will send a curse on you, and I will curse your blessings. Yes, I have already cursed them, because you have not resolved to honor me'" (NIV). Wow. As believers, when we don't acknowledge who God is in our lives and the abilities He has gifted us with, we are walking in disobedience, away from His blessings. We can easily fall prey to this in our marriages, in our work, in our passions, in our parenting, and in any area of life. When we do something for our glory and gain, even if we think we are being humble, we are really just deceiving ourselves into thinking we are that amazing on our own. We elevate ourselves above God.

Once we believe in Jesus, success will look different to us. Our eyes will be set on eternity. Therefore, everything we do—whether in word, deed, or thought—will reflect that goal. What we accomplish might not look as glorious as an Olympic athlete winning gold, but I guarantee you that standing in the presence of God and hearing the words "Well done, good and faithful servant!" (Matthew 25:23, NIV) will be far better than any earthly award. Don't take it from me, though—take it from the Word of God, which tells us this: "No, dear brothers and sisters, I have not achieved it, but I focus on this one thing: Forgetting the past and looking forward to what lies ahead, I press on to reach the end of the race and receive the heavenly prize for which God, through Christ Jesus, is calling us" (Philippians 3:13-14).

Our aim every day should be to ask God for the strength to complete what He has put before us. If that's keeping up a household with lots of little kids running around, amen! If that's running a race on a worldwide stage for all to see, amen! When both are done in the strength of the Lord, the goal is the same: eternal life! We each have a path to follow, and as long as we keep God at the forefront, we will be equipped to do what He has called us to do.

Let's walk forward into this week thanking God for the abilities He has given us. Ask the Lord to show you any areas where you have been trying to succeed in your own strength. When He answers, be willing to repent and proclaim His name and strength over that area of your life. Proclaim the name of Jesus in all you do, and know that in everything, we can and should choose to give glory where glory is due.

Pray

Dear Lord, thank You that You created me to serve You in all I do. I acknowledge that everything I have, whether little or much, is a gift from You. Help me keep a right spirit and attitude for the things You have set before me. Whether it's everyday tasks or huge projects, I want to have the same approach: living for You and for the Kingdom of Heaven. Help me not to get caught up in the ways of the world that promote "me first" attitudes. I want to focus on You alone, which means I need You, God. I need You to be part of my whole life. I ask You to strengthen me each day and equip me to do Your will. When I'm weak, I know that You are always my strength. Help me to encourage others to turn to You as well, and let my life be a testimony of Your goodness and faithfulness to me in all circumstances. I love You, Lord, and I can't wait to be in heaven one day with You! In Jesus' name, amen.

Everything
she does
comes from
the overflow
of her heart.

50

Clothed with Strength and Dignity

Her children stand and bless her. Her husband praises her: "There are many virtuous and capable women in the world, but you surpass them all!"

PROVERBS 31:28-29

FROM THE TIME I WAS YOUNG, I was a natural at nurturing. I took care of my animals, lined up my stuffies, eventually babysat for other people's children, and even nannied for a couple of summers. I knew I wanted to be a mother someday. I remember serving in our church nursery with all the babies and toddlers when I was fifteen. Another woman who served in the nursery was a labor and delivery nurse. She told me story after story about her job and how much she loved helping bring new life into the world. I was hooked. Now, along with wanting to be a wife and mother, I had the ambition to become a nurse. Even though I knew nursing would be a wonderful career, I ultimately wanted to be a stay-at-home mom and move nursing to a backup plan should we ever need it. Over the next several years, all those dreams became a reality. I loved motherhood. Then I began reading about the Proverbs 31 woman. Whew! She is something, isn't she? I realized I had a lot to learn, and it started to feel unattainable.

There were times in those early years (and even now) where my love for motherhood got overshadowed by all the to-dos. And in the middle of it all, I was supposed to be a Proverbs 31 woman too? I mean, she does things like finding wool and flax and spinning it. She inspects a field, buys it with her earnings, and plants a vineyard. She is strong, energetic, and hardworking, making her own bedspreads and getting dressed in fine linen and purple gowns. She brings her food from afar, and I'm just trying to figure out at 4 p.m. what's for dinner tonight. It feels lofty to think that, in the midst of doing the dishes, changing diapers, and picking up toys, we are somehow supposed to live up to the standards set in Proverbs 31.

But I'd like to step back and submit a different perspective on the Proverbs 31 woman. When the Bible says, "She makes her own bedspreads" (verse 22), does that mean we need to take up sewing and spend our days outfitting our family? When the Bible says, "She goes to inspect a field and buys it; with her earnings she plants a vineyard" (verse 16), does that mean all of us need to work outside the home? Not exactly. When the Bible speaks on the Proverbs 31 woman, what we learn isn't just about what she does but who she is inside. Everything she does comes from the overflow of her heart. If we spend our days as wives and mothers in a posture of lack and work from a deficit mentally, physically, and spiritually, we aren't going to be able to pour into our family the way God calls us to.

The Proverbs 31 woman models strength, wisdom, and dedication to her family and community. She has high moral standards. You might not be in charge of profitable business dealings, but you may be discipling your children in matters of the heart, which pays lifelong dividends. You might not be spinning thread, but maybe you are balancing the budget and making wise choices for your resources. You can walk with dignity knowing that the choices you make for your family reflect what the Lord is doing in your heart. You can speak words that are wise and give instructions to your children with kindness. We are capable of doing everything with the Lord's help in a way that honors Him and honors our family.

Whatever circumstances God has put us in define our calling. God chose you for your calling because He knew you could do it. The best part is He doesn't make you do it alone. The tasks we do in our home when no one sees are sometimes the ones that bear the most fruit. We don't have to compare ourselves to others when we know what God has called us to. We just have to learn to keep our eyes on Jesus, which shifts our focus away from what others are doing. And when we mess up or misstep, God gently guides us back to His path of life.

Don't let past mistakes or less-than days define your entire journey. Not even the tough spots of motherhood can hold us back when we invite the Lord into our struggles. When we allow Him to change our hearts, He makes them beautiful and satisfied in Him. When our hearts are satisfied in the Lord, our strength tank is full, and we can bless others and make a difference in our homes.

If you are a mother of little ones, God has called you to a life that doesn't always look glamorous on the outside—especially when you have spit-up staining your favorite shirt. But the reward and richness that come with the motherhood calling leave a lasting legacy in the hearts of your children and their children as well. And this legacy goes far beyond our lives on earth. When we live rightly before the Lord, we are also training our children up in the way they should go so that, as they grow older, they don't stray from it (see Proverbs 22:6). Yes, our children have to make their own choice to follow Jesus. We can't do it for them. But as moms, we get the opportunity to aim them in the right direction. We have the high calling to launch them for the Lord and do it with dignity, strength, and wisdom.

Let's walk forward into this week asking the Lord to stretch us. Prayer should be our best friend. If we have been working from a deficit, let's ask God for wisdom and practical tips. Maybe it's a new type of budgeting or waking up a little earlier. With the Lord's help, we can choose to start fresh and become the type of woman, wife, and mother He calls us to be.

Pray

Dear Lord, thank You for designing the role of motherhood with care and gifting each mother with the unique ability to bless her family. I want to serve my family with Your love at the forefront of all I do. Lord, help me to keep my eyes focused on You and not turn to the left or the right. Thank You for giving me exactly what I need to accomplish Your will as a mother. Help me to be the caretaker, meal maker, home cleaner, master snuggler, on-my-knees pray-er, and everything else I need to be to keep my family surrendered to You daily. Lord, I want to be like the Proverbs 31 woman, clothed in your strength and dignity. Help me to be wise with my words and kind with my instructions. Help me to model Your love well to the children I'm blessed to raise. And give me strength to support my husband as he fulfills his calling with integrity. In Jesus' name, amen.

Nothing is
going to
change until
we make
the call.

51

Check Engine Light

Search me, O God, and know my heart;
test me and know my anxious thoughts.
Point out anything in me that offends you,
and lead me along the path of everlasting life.

PSALM 139:23–24

"HOW LONG HAS THE CHECK ENGINE LIGHT BEEN ON?" Tim asked me as we were driving in town.

To which I replied honestly, "I don't know. I didn't even really notice."

"Babe, it's really important to do something when that light comes on. We need to take it in and find out what's wrong."

I shrugged my shoulders, knowing he was right but also feeling like that wasn't my department. I kind of hoped the light would just turn off on its own. You know, fix itself. But that is usually wishful thinking. Those check engine lights come on for a reason. If we ignored the light, our car might run for a little while longer with no problems. But eventually something would happen, and chances were the problem would be a much bigger and more expensive issue than if we had just taken it in right away.

As we were driving home, I felt such a clear voice in my spirit. *You also have a check engine light in life, Sarah. Have you looked at your relationship with the Lord lately?* I pondered that thought the whole way home and into the evening. What is my responsibility? What happens when I get the check engine light and shrug it off, thinking it will solve itself? I know that voice when I hear it. The Holy Spirit gently reminding me of wisdom for everyday living. Not letting me forget that my life isn't meant just for me, and I can't just go through each day on autopilot. In this particular season, I knew I was on autopilot with the Lord.

I was anticipating that God would continue to carry me through (which He did) but neglecting to take the time to check in with Him and make sure I was on the path He laid out for me. And that I was walking that path with my whole heart.

Much like on our cars, our check engine light is there to help alert us of an issue that needs to be, well, checked up on. What is our check engine light? It's the check we feel inside when something is off. I believe this usually comes from the Holy Spirit. The One that helps us discern and have wisdom in everyday living. The Spirit alerts us that a problem has been detected and, although the issue could be minor or major, we need to address it as soon as possible. Because if we don't, minor can turn to major real quick. Have you had situations like that in life, whether on your own or with other people? Something happens, either with someone else or just yourself. You think, *Eh, I'll take care of that next week.* For example, maybe you had a tense conversation with a family member or friend that was left unresolved. And you know you need to go back to finish that conversation even though it would be a whole lot easier to just ignore it and try to move on. But here's the problem with that mentality. Instead of nipping something in the bud and clearing it out, we let it grow like a weed. And just like a weed, it grows quickly and soon causes more problems than if we had just addressed it right away.

So how do we address these check engine lights in ourselves? First, read the Bible and get back into a daily relationship with God. Second, talk to God! Pray throughout the day, inviting God into everything that happens in your life. While praying, ask the Lord to show you any areas that you have neglected to take care of. If there are, ask forgiveness from any offended party and also God. Sin grieves him too.

Ephesians 4:30 says, "Do not bring sorrow to God's Holy Spirit by the way you live. Remember, he has identified you as his own, guaranteeing that you will be saved on the day of redemption." Thank goodness for the Holy Spirit, who is gracious and kind not only to be our Advocate and Helper in life but also to alert us when something is off and reveal any areas that might need a tune-up.

We just need to be aware that once those areas are revealed, it's our responsibility to repair and restore them. When we don't obey, we slowly slip into sin and out of freedom with Christ. James 1:23-25 puts it best: "If you listen to the word and don't obey, it is like glancing at your face in a mirror. You see yourself, walk away, and forget what you look like. But if you look carefully into the perfect law that sets you free, and if you do what it says and don't forget what you heard, then God will bless you for doing it."

Nothing is going to change until we make the call. When our lives need a tune-up, we can try to walk away. But somehow, someway, we will eventually find our way back to Jesus. The question is: Will we have wasted valuable time ignoring what needs to be done in our lives? If so, we may be like James described, looking in the mirror someday only to forget immediately what we saw. But staying in the hard seasons and looking to Jesus to pull you through and make a way out, that is when we find true freedom and blessing from the Lord. And one thing we know about God's blessings is that they are far more than anything we could think up ourselves. Amen to that!

Let's walk forward into this week and ask the Lord to do a tune-up in our lives. It doesn't have to be a big production. Just ask God to reveal any areas of sin that could be keeping us from moving forward into what He has for us. Then let's be willing to take action to get back to where we need to be. We can seek God by putting in the work of reading our Bible, praying, and listening for His voice. These practical steps will have a direct effect on every other area of our lives.

Pray

Dear Lord, thank You that I don't have to do life on my own. Thank You that You've sent the Holy Spirit to be my Counselor, Advocate, Helper, Comforter, Teacher, Intercessor, and Guide. I don't want to walk through life obliviously, not taking care of my spirit the way You want me to. I want to be diligent to keep in step with Your will for my life. Lord, would You give me wisdom to make the right changes at the right time that help me to run at the pace You've laid out for me? Make me aware of any blind spots so I can be on alert and ready for anything. Surround me with people who help keep my eyes and heart focused on You. And when I mess up, help me to seek forgiveness quickly. I want to run my race well rather than sputtering to the finish line. Thank You for keeping my mind in perfect peace. I trust in You! In Jesus' name, amen.

Only one thing guarantees eternal life: saying yes to Jesus.

52

No Regrets

Jesus told him, "I am the way, the truth, and the life. No one can come to the Father except through me."

JOHN 14:6

WE'VE WALKED THROUGH a lot together throughout this book. But I've learned that we can give and receive all the encouragement in the world, and it still doesn't guarantee eternity. Only one thing guarantees eternal life: saying yes to Jesus. When I was working on my first book, I told my publishers that I felt there was no more appropriate way to end than by sharing the story of what God has done in my life. From the first yes that I said to Jesus at age five to all the continual yeses since, I have never once regretted my decision to follow Jesus and ask Him to be King over my life. I want to share about that with you now.

I remember one time Tim and I were asking our doctor questions about having more children. He had a larger family himself and loved the Lord with all his heart. He said something that was so impactful to me at the time: we would never regret the children we have, but we may regret the children we didn't have. I can tell you that same concept applies when it comes to the Lord. You will never regret your decision to say yes to Jesus and live a life following Him. The God we serve will never fail you. He is the same generation after generation. Psalm 119:89-91 says, "Your eternal word, O LORD, stands firm in heaven. Your faithfulness extends to *every* generation, as enduring as the earth you created. Your regulations remain true to this day, for *everything serves your plans*" (emphasis added). We can choose to stand outside of God's plans, or we can choose to be on the inside, where hearts are shifting and heaven is being packed out.

Life is exciting with Jesus. Not the fleeting type of excitement that felt good in the moment but when you wake up the next morning you feel shame and wonder what you have done. Rather, it's the type of excitement that gets you out of bed each morning wondering, *What are we going to do today, Jesus?* because you know you serve a God who gives you a place in His plans! That's the God we serve and the type of Kingdom I want to be a part of. A God of purpose, a God of intention, a God who is faithful, a God who is just, a God who is all-knowing, a God who is present with us, a God who is our counselor, a God who is our friend, a God who is our creator, a God who formed us in our mother's womb and thought of us long before earth was even created, a God who is so much more than we could write in the pages of a book.

It's easy to talk about all the goodness of God, but I also want to talk about His redemption. When we make a mistake in life, we can try to hold ourselves accountable, but we aren't reliable. We change our mind as quickly as the weather changes. The same goes for our feelings. Feelings, although God given and fulfilling an important role, can be fickle. They aren't the be-all and end-all in our lives. We often put too much stock in them, which never turns out well. When I was single and really hoping to get married, I decided to take things into my own hands instead of letting God's plans play out for my life. I started dating someone I knew didn't align with my morals and values, let alone align with God's. I was so antsy to get to where I wanted to be that I began to convince myself I could make things happen if I just tried hard enough. Thankfully, before I compromised myself, the Lord intervened on my behalf. I got out of that relationship quickly and met my husband days later. I can't begin to imagine what my life would've looked like had I forced my own way. I can tell you this: it would've been one compromise at a time that led down a slippery slope of turning my back on the things of the Lord. Goodness, I'm thankful God saved me from that!

Rest assured that when you turn your life over to the Lord, it will get turned upside down but in the best way possible. It won't be perfect or easy, but when you go through hard times, you can take every thought and care to Him. You will begin to see everything through the lens of God's purposes and plans, and suddenly all that you had planned out for yourself will look unappealing compared to what the Lord promises. The best part? Life with Jesus is free to those who ask. It's as simple as just saying yes to Jesus, welcoming Him in, and asking Him to clean out our hearts and forgive our sins. Romans 10:9 says, "If you openly declare that Jesus is Lord and believe in your heart that God raised him from the dead, you will be saved."

Not everyone will welcome the good news of Jesus, but I pray you do. After all that God has done in my life—the miracles I have seen and all He has walked me out of and through—the least I can do is honor Him with my life and choose to share His name with everyone I get to meet here on earth!

Let's walk forward into this week saying yes to Jesus. Whether it's your first yes (yay!) or a recommitting yes (also yay!), say it out loud and tell Jesus that you believe in Him, want Him to forgive you, and invite Him into your heart and life. When you do this, you'll never regret it. You will be saved! Praise Jesus. And beyond that, seek to connect with a church locally, and if you know a Christian friend or family member, reach out and ask them to celebrate and support your newfound life in Christ! You aren't meant to live this Christian life alone. To finish well but also begin again, let's pray one more time together just as we have done every other time before.

Pray

Dear Lord, thank You for always being with me even when I haven't acknowledged You. I want You to be the most important thing in my life, and I'm ready to say yes to You! Please forgive me for the times I have sinned and even used Your name in a way that wasn't honoring. Come into my heart and clean out all the junk that doesn't bring You glory or help me live fully. I ask You to fill those empty spaces with Your love and purposes for my life. I openly declare that Jesus is Lord and Savior over my life and that I want Him living in my heart. Come live in my heart, Jesus. Thank You for dying on the cross and willingly taking on all my sin. I believe that You defeated death, and because of this I want to live eternal life with You! Lord, help me start fresh and turn my life around so everything I do begins to reflect Your goodness in my life. I love You, Jesus! In Jesus' name, amen.

Acknowledgments

DEAR LORD—What an honor it is to be able to write this. I don't take it lightly. Thank You for giving me the opportunity and the people in my life to help make it something that will honor and glorify You and hopefully draw people closer to You! I'm humbled by everything You place in my lap and will always honor You with it all. All my life You have been faithful. I love You, Lord!

To my hunk, Tim—You made this happen (as you do with everything) through your encouragement, your willingness to let me go write, and your "Come on, you're so close" cheering me on. You're my favorite person ever. Thank you for cheering me on not only with this devo but also in every area of life. I can always count on you and I always do. You are my best friend. I love you so much! —Your Sweet

To the best Dad and Mom—Thanks for always letting me call you, text you, FaceTime you, and pick your brain on what you like and don't like in devotionals, as well as chatting all things Bible and the Lord. You have always aimed to prefer and pour into others, and I'm forever inspired to do the same because of your influence and the way you live out what you believe! Your wisdom and humor, along with your encouragement, make me feel like the most loved daughter in the world. I know I am! Love you both!

Dearest Kara, aka best publisher ever—Round 2 complete! And nobody I'd rather publish this devotional with (I mean that!). You are more than just a publisher; you are a friend. I love that our "meetings" start with catching up on life and at any given moment (see what I did there?) can include a child or seven who want to say hi to Miss Kara. You are loved by all of us. And you are great at making this process feel so smooth. Thank you from the bottom of my heart for trusting me and giving me this opportunity. So much love for you!

To the coolest and best sisters, Rachel, Micah, and Caitlin—You guys are always so faithful to respond when I crowdsource and send a whole load of texts asking opinions and questions on wording, colors, covers, and more. Don't ever get sick of it, because I count on you. The best sisters and best friends a girl could ask for—that's YOU! Even more than that, you're examples of women who truly love the Lord, love the Word of God, and love others well. I look up to each of you, and I'm so glad you are the ones God gave me. Love each of you so much!

To my dear Eden—Goodness, what a gift you are to not only our family but to me. You are truly family and stuck with us now. Thank you for being a dear friend and someone I can chat with about all the things. And I mean ALL of them! You graciously let me show you all the sneak peeks and steps and willingly give me your opinion, which I love! Thank you for holding down the fort so many afternoons during naptime while I crammed in writing or snuck into another room for a meeting. I am so grateful for who you are to us! God plopped you in our family, and I hope you always feel welcome and loved. I love you!

To Danika, who is a whiz of an editor—I don't know how you do it, but you never cease to amaze me with your ability to whittle down what I give you and make it sound so eloquent and put together. I'll forever be grateful for your giftings because without them, this book might be thirty extra pages of mumbo jumbo. Also thank you for being such a kind and sweet spirit who sprinkles grace with every word you say whenever we talk. I'm grateful for you and all you contributed to make this devotional the best it can be. All my love and thanks!

Judy/Mom 2—You have prayed endlessly for me as I write, and I feel each prayer. The way you encourage me is as if I were your own daughter. I'm so proud to be your daughter-in-love and thankful for a bonus mom who spurs me on in the ways of the Lord. Love you!

My IG friends—This book was inspired by each of you. Those of you who show up week in and week out for our Sunday night prayers (and have been there since the beginning) and those of you who pop in once in a while. It all means so much to me. This book was born out of those nights, and I hope they feel like an extension of encouragement that you can always take with you. Thanks for encouraging me to keep it up, knowing that God is always reaching the heart of at least one person. May the words I speak be His . . . not my own. You friends are the best online community a girl could possibly have!

Index

A

Answered Prayers *5*
Anxiety *9, 25*
Arguments *55*
Armor of God *17, 119, 171*

B

Being Present *95*
Burdens *13, 25*

C

Calling *91, 127, 143, 149, 189, 217, 229, 235, 241*
Change *35*
Character *41, 107, 143, 211*
Choices *143*
Clarity *21, 35*
Communication *55, 183, 223*
Community *51, 193, 205*
Companions *21*
Comparison *75, 149, 241*
Confession *103, 167*
Conflict *55, 193*
Consistency *205*
Control *13, 55, 163, 189*
Courage *9, 45, 63, 143, 217*
Crisis *9*

D

Decisions *99, 143, 189, 211*
Dependence *45, 193, 205, 235*
Dependence on God *5, 25, 115*
Depression *25, 199*
Desires *179*
Despair *25*
Diligence *127, 205*
Direction *35, 99*
Discernment *21, 55, 99, 123, 171, 211, 247*
Discipline *163, 205*
Discouragement *5*
Disobedience *103, 123, 127*
Dreams *79, 143, 235*

E

Emotions *85, 163, 253*
Encouragement *51, 153, 157, 163, 183, 193*
Eternity *35, 79, 127, 175, 205, 235*
Exhaustion *13*

F
Faith 63, 69, 175, 217
Family 51, 115, 175, 183
Fear 9, 35, 45, 63, 111
Feelings 85, 163, 205, 253
Flexibility 95
Following God 143, 253
Forgiveness 103, 167
Friendship 25, 51, 55, 179, 199
Frustration 17
Fulfillment 127

G
Gifts 91, 127, 153, 217, 235
Goals 75, 79, 107, 115, 235
God's Character 85
God's Faithfulness 5, 9, 119, 123, 133
God's Goodness 9
God's Love 179
God's Presence 9, 45
God's Voice 21, 123, 139, 229
God's Will 99, 119, 127, 189
God's Word 17, 21, 25, 31, 45, 85, 111, 205, 211, 229
Good Fruit 41, 91, 95, 107, 149, 205, 211
Grace 99, 149
Gratitude 149, 235
Grief 199
Growth 41, 75, 149, 163, 167, 217
Guidance 21, 63, 123, 189, 247
Guilt 103

H
Habits 205
Healing 5, 199
Heaven 35, 127
Holiness 211
Holy Spirit 21, 45, 115, 133, 139, 167, 211, 247
Honesty 103, 167
Hope 9

I
Identity 153
Inner Beauty 41, 107
Integrity 171
Intercession 115

J
Joy 95, 103, 211, 217

K
Kindness 157, 183, 193
Knowing God 85, 205
Knowledge 99

L
Leadership 45
Legacy 51, 175, 241
Listening 223
Loss 199
Love 193, 199
Loving God 5, 179, 193
Loving Others 51, 157, 183, 193, 199

M
Marriage 55, 179, 183, 223
Mental Health 25
Mentors 205
Mercy 75
Miracles 69

O
Obedience 45, 59, 63, 79, 115, 123, 127, 133, 167, 171, 175, 189, 193, 211, 217

P
Panic 9, 45
Parenting 107, 153, 175, 199, 229, 241
Peace 9, 55, 95, 119, 149, 179
Perseverance 45, 205
Perspective 35, 45, 107, 119, 127, 199
Plans 95, 115, 143, 189
Praise 9
Prayer 133, 139, 205, 223, 241, 247
Preparation 17, 223
Priorities 115
Protection 5, 17, 171
Purification 167
Purpose 91, 119, 127, 149, 153, 179, 189, 217, 235

R
Redemption 199, 253
Relationships 55, 143, 163, 179, 183, 193, 199, 223, 229
Relationship with God 21, 115, 133, 139, 179, 247
Repentance 103, 167
Rescue 5
Rest 13, 59, 119
Restoration 199

S
Seasons 149, 189
Security 123
Self-Control 163, 183
Serving Others 91, 157, 183, 217
Sin 211
Spiritual Warfare 17, 111, 119, 171, 223
Strength 45, 211, 235
Struggles 25
Suffering 199
Surrender 9, 13, 107, 119, 167

T
The Enemy 17, 171, 223
Time Management 59, 95, 115
Timing 75, 157
Transformation 41, 139
Trust 5, 35, 63, 107, 119, 123, 133, 189, 205
Truth 21, 31, 111, 205, 229

U
Uncertainty 9, 35, 63, 111, 217
Understanding 99

V
Vigilance 17, 223
Vision 35, 133
Vulnerability 199

W
Weariness 13, 59, 149
Wisdom 55, 79, 99, 123, 163, 171, 183, 189, 193, 205, 211, 229, 241, 247
Words 183, 223
Work 59, 127
Worry 107

About the Author

SARAH MOLITOR is a wife, mom to seven kids, and author. She has a passion for serving others and enjoys authentically and consistently engaging with her growing social media community, where she encourages, challenges, and inspires women daily. Sarah connects with individuals all over the world, frequently sharing bits of her family, home, and everyday life. She loves candy (but dislikes chocolate) and finds extra joy in homeschooling and hosting others. Visit Sarah online at modernfarmhousefamily.com and on Instagram @modernfarmhousefamily.